the
Journey
Principles™
YOUR JOURNEY, GOD'S PRINCIPLES

THE JOURNEY™ PRINCIPLES

10 Simple Principles for a Life Journey that Matters

by

Stephen Scoggins

©2014

Stephen Scoggins Publishing
1001 Corporation Parkway Suite 112
Raleigh, NC 27610
www.stephenscoggins.com

Ordering information: Quantity sales. Special discounts are available on quantity purchases by corporations, associations, and others. For details, contact the publisher at the address above. Orders on-line with various trade bookstores and wholesalers such as Amazon: www.amazon.com.

Printed in the United States of America

The Journey Principles: 10 Journey Principles / Stephen Scoggins.
ISBN10:   0990979008
ISBN13:   978-0-9909790-0-5
Non-fiction: Motivational, Self-Help and Spiritual. First Edition

This book is not a substitute for the medical advice of a physician or therapist. The reader should regularly consult a physician in matters relating to his/her health and particularly with respect to any symptoms that may require diagnosis or medical attention. Although the author and publisher have made every effort to ensure that the information in this book was correct at press time, the author and publisher do not assume and hereby disclaim any liability to any party. The intent of the author is only to offer information of a general nature to help you in your quest for spiritual fitness and good health. In the event you use any of the information in this book for yourself, which is your constitutional right, the author and the publisher assume no responsibility for your actions.

Cover photograph by Kate Kucharzyk
Cover design by Jeff Lawson, Cowan Graphic Design, Inc.
Book design and production by Wendy Muse Greenwood, Inspiration FX,
www.inspirationfx.org

This book is dedicated to all of the Custom Home Exteriors teams. Thank you for your dreams, ambitions, and for letting me practice life-giving messages in and over your lives. There is no team like a CHE TEAM, "GORWTH HOLA"!! [sic]

This book is dedicated to you – the *Reader*. You are brave. You are awesome. The fact that you have decided to bring a positive change into your life is a blessed decision.

"As a man thinketh in his heart so shall he be."

James Allen, As a Man Thinketh

I believe in you, your heart, your mind and your soul! Most importantly, I believe in what you can become by facing your journey head on no matter the twists, the turns, the hills, and/or the valleys. No matter where your journey leads you, inspire others to embrace the beautiful truths they will learn from the adversities in life. Believe in others.

Go inspire someone!

Acknowledgements

It's funny to think about acknowledgements. As I sit to write this, I am humbled by all who have played a part of this journey. The truth is, I am not sure I could correctly and accurately give the proper thanks to all those who inspired me before, during and after *The Journey Principles* came to life.

I will give it my all to offer some special thanks to those special friends, mentors, and believers. We all need that one person who believes in us, and helps move us closer to our purpose, dreams, and callings. My journey started with one, but as I look up and around me, I realize I'm surrounded by incredible people who are living their own special journeys.

First and foremost, I give all praise and glory to my creator God and honor to my Lord and Savior, Jesus Christ. I thank Him for this walk and all these lessons and the man He has created me to be. I pledge to continue this course and to always do my best, to learn each day, and to share the grace and mercy God has shown me with others.

> *"It was the pain of the refinement that gave me the joy of the journey, and I am forever yours, Lord. Thank You, Lord Jesus, for your sacrifice, use me as you will. I exalt thee."*
> *-S. Scoggins*

To all of those who have brought life-giving messages to me: you mean the world to me and you know who you are.

Acknowledgements

I have so many special thanks to offer so I will start from those that gave me life. My Grandfather George Stallings aka "The Silver Fox", I humbly thank you for speaking life over me (when my heart was searching for death). I give thanks that you led me to the altar of the Lord. You have played a part in my eternal resting place and my commitment. I thank my two grandmothers: for starters, "Nanny" Barbra Oakley, for helping to raise me as my parents struggled, for teaching me about unconditional love, and for giving that love to me, a love that I could see and feel. I then remember these words from my 4'11" firecracker of grandmother, Christine Scoggins, when she said, "Stephen, good things come in small packages, but more importantly, so does dynamite. You can be great if you just want to." Those words helped me more than she was ever able to witness before heading off to Heaven herself. Love and gratitude to both of my parents, Glenn Scoggins and Donna Stallings, for their love and encouragement. I am so incredibly happy to see you both having successful journeys of your own and how your journeys' prepared me for mine.

Steve Myrick (who was like a father to me), his words have stuck with me each day of my life: "Stephen, do today what others won't, so you can have tomorrow what others don't!" I cannot say enough about Susan Batts, except this: you clothed me, you fed me, and mentored me and I wasn't even yours. I remember you each and every day and how you answered the phone as I looked on the traffic below. Without you and your wise words - "This too shall pass" - there would be no *Journey Principles*, no CHE, and most of all, no me. You are an angel from God Himself, and you will forever be my Mamawama! I want to extend a special thank you to regional distributors Revere Building Products. I want to especially thank Frank Weisner and Mark Bernhardt for the risk you both took in a virtually homeless twenty-something kid with really big dreams. Thank you for believing in me long before others, or even I, saw it in me. Your mentoring has made a huge impact in my life. To Michelle Sealy, my sister and friend in Christ: you have meant so much to me. You helped me break out of my divorce stupor and helped me navigate some crazy waters. You led me to my Journey back from anxiety. Thank you so much for your patience and encouragement. Thank you for believing in the leader God has asked me to grow into and for being my very first speaking engagement.

Dave Ramsey and team, you rock! EntreLeadership team, I can't thank you all enough for showing an organization with heart how to define its direction. Thank you for also showing that not only does the business matter, the people do too. Thank you for the vision to build a company and people with meaningful work that matters! It's funny looking back to how EntreLeadership led me to what would be a lifelong friend in Chris LoCurto (chrislocurto.com). I am very thankful for you, Chris. I remember all too well how there was no time on your calendar to help a broken hearted business owner over his next hurdle, but how you gave me your personal time to mentor and encourage me. I am so thankful for your new business in teaching others about Life Plan, a way to understand how God's handprint over our lives helps us gain perspective and insight that includes an understanding of the Journey for the life to come. You have been an awesome friend, mentor, and coach. You were at your best because you were willing to get your hands dirty in helping me and others. God has great plans for you! Thank You, Rebecca Henderson, for your top line editing and helping to find Mrs. Wendy Muse to get past my numerous grammar and spelling challenges. Thank you to Jeff Lawson and to Cowan Graphic Design for your awesome graphic art/design for this cover and future publications. I want to extend a special thank you to Wendy Muse Greenwood, Program, Curriculum & Project Director with InspirationFX.org, for your continued ideas and for getting the book into the hands of those who desire its contents and teachings.

Love and gratitude to my beautiful and life-giving fiancé, Karen Smith. Your love and support have brought a new level of encouragement and grace into my life. You love and encourage with ease; the only thing bigger than your ability to inspire is your faith in God. No words can express what you bring into my life. I Love you!

Table of Contents

Prologue

It's been said that suicide is a selfish act and I agree. In late 1997, I was sitting on an overpass in Raleigh, North Carolina. I wasn't thinking about my friends, family, or any of the wonderful relationships with which God had blessed me. There was no highlight reel of memories playing before my eyes. I simply watched through the blur of streaming tears and wondered which of the numerous vehicles whirring beneath me would finish the job.

That day was not just another day in the life of Stephen Scoggins. It was supposed to be the day that everything changed for the better. I had spent the last eight months training for the military and hopefully had earned the opportunity to enter into the Navy which was to lead to the SEAL training program. That day I had a late afternoon appointment at the Military Entrance Processing Station (MEPS) where I was to receive my assignment and deploy.

I was sitting in a small processing office feeling a little anxious and excited. I was extremely serious about starting my new life. When the MEPS processing agent came into the room, he was wearing his Navy whites. His hair was dark and slicked back sort of like Tom Cruise in "A Few Good Men," complete with the oversized honker.

He explained that, thanks to my GED, I had barely passed the Armed Services Vocational Aptitude Battery (ASVAB) entry test. He told me even if the test had gone differently, they had found a slight trace of scoliosis at the top of my spine which would prevent me from ever being able to become a SEAL.

He was very matter-of-fact and offered no comfort or sympathy. In a few words, he had crushed my plans for the future and confirmed a lifelong belief that I would never measure up, that I would never be good enough, and that I wasn't going anywhere.

I walked out of the MEPS office in a daze. Oblivious to anything that was taking place around me, I could not comprehend the fact that I was unable to make it into the military. They take anyone willing to sign their name on the line, yet here I was failing at such a simple task.

I began to walk for what felt like hours, sinking back into the depression that had led me to make the decision to go into the military in the first place. I was walking down Capitol Boulevard in Raleigh when I came to the overpass that overlooked highway 440, an eight-lane highway and one of the busiest in the city. I crawled up the cement structure and took a seat on the metal railing. My senses were overwhelmed. The excitement that had filled the air earlier that day was replaced with diesel fumes. Honking cars drowned out all sound as they tried their best to prevent me from taking that empty step forward. My vision was hazy, blurred by the wetness of my tears. I felt numb and the only thing I could taste was failure.

Then something changed. Everything became quiet and all of the hectic commotions surrounding me became still. For the first time, I wasn't thinking of myself. Something was speaking to me and telling me that there were people who were going to be affected by my decision and that I needed to reach out to them to let them know what they had meant to me and that I would miss them. There was no audible voice speaking to me; it was more like an urging, an unseen impulse pushing me not off the overpass, but back into my life, back into the relationships that were my only source of meaning.

I tried to call my father, but there was no answer at his house. I tried to call my grandfather, but the phone was busy. I called Susan "The Original Mamawama" and she answered...

~~~~~~~

The pages that follow are not just a biography, the story of a man who was virtually homeless and suicidal and is now the owner of a few successful businesses, the most successful of which is a multimillion-dollar corporation. No, not just that. My prayer is that you will find these principles to be inspirational and motivational. I hope that my journey can, in some way, help you as you discover your path. It is my belief that no matter what your personal calling may be, we are all created to love and serve one another as we experience life together and face its many adversities.

Obstacles are not simply something that you go through, around, or over. When you truly confront and overcome an obstacle, it becomes a part of you and functions as a teaching tool that not only helps you define who you are as an individual, but also helps you perceive and take action in the world. If the principles of your obstacles are left in your wake, you will most likely end up tripping over them again later in life. However, if you own them and make them yours, then those obstacles, like bricks, can be used to lay the foundation for success.

The ten principles of this book explore ten very specific obstacles that I've faced in my life. The Journey Principles will help you construct a foundation for success, but I want to be clear that finding success does not mean that you will find happiness. It is true that with more money comes more problems. Despite the financial security that a prosperous business has provided, I have only been able to find true happiness and comfort resting in the love of my Lord and Savior, Jesus Christ. While running a company presents worthwhile challenges and responsibilities, I take the most joy in helping others ignite their passions and in glorifying my Father by using His blessings to bless others.

> *"The great thing, if one can, is to stop regarding all the unpleasant things as interruptions of one's 'own,' or 'real life."* -C.S. Lewis

The truth is, of course, that what one calls interruptions are precisely one's real life, the life God is sending day by day. My life is still full of adversity, but my approach has changed. I no longer look at obstacles as something that I must overcome, but as a chance to grow ever closer to God. You must face despair to know hope. Without doubt, you will never know faith. Until you experience the darkness, you will not be able to distinguish the light.

Be blessed,
Stephen

Journey Principle 1: "Understanding Life's Conflicts"

Prayer

Father in Heaven, please show me guidance, wisdom, and understanding. Please reveal to me the purpose behind the conflicts of my life and how they are meant to build your kingdom and purpose for my life. Please allow me the grace to see the pain points in my life and your handprints on them. Prepare my path of healing. In Jesus' name, amen.

Stephen Scoggins

1

Journey Principle 1:
"Understanding Life's Conflicts"

Ask any writer and they will tell you that the driving force of the story is conflict. Why? Because without conflict, there is no story. Is it because controversy and struggle create tension and excitement for the reader? I would suggest that beyond simply being entertained, most people desire a resolution that involves change and growth. Conflict is the genesis of growth. It is the instrument that pushes us to explore our feelings, shape our beliefs, and ultimately create our definition of self. If you read the prologue, you know that I define myself by who I am in Christ. It is with and through Jesus Christ that I can tell you about the conflicts in my life that helped me better understand my Father's mercy and grace. Conflict draws me closer to Him. You may not share my faith, but know that it is the friction in your life that makes you who you are. Conflict can make you stronger.

In literature, conflict is usually described as being internal or external. I think that this approach is just as applicable in the story of our lives. Internal conflict is how an individual processes things within their mind, be it psychologically or philosophically. External conflict is one's experience with outside forces or the surrounding world. It usually describes our relationships and contact with others. It can also include other influences such as weather (elements) or time (place/culture/era). For this book, I want to focus solely on the relationship aspect of external conflict because I am a firm believer in letting go of that which is outside of my control. I am learning to place those worries in the hands of God and trust that "all things work together for the good of those that have been called according to His purpose" (Romans 8:28).

That is a simple statement, but not a simple process. Some of the strongest believers that I know still have trouble relinquishing control, but I can promise you it becomes easier and easier when you do. Again, you may not share my beliefs, but let me urge you to practice letting go. The stresses of life can be debilitating if you waste time worrying about what you cannot control. Internal and external conflict has one thing in common: they both present you with the opportunity to make a choice. Life is a series of choices and no matter what you tell yourself you believe, it is your choices that *will* define you. Now every single person in the world has developed their concept of morality: right or wrong, good or evil. Even so, most people will tell you that they do not believe that life is as simple as right or wrong and that you must operate in shades of grey. I disagree. I believe that life is as simple as choosing or not choosing God. There are no shades of grey when seeking His will.

Well, Stephen, what about those of us who do not believe in God? I'm glad you asked! I have met so many people who, in their worldview, also believe there are no shades of grey and that life's broken down into two choices: love or fear. Whether you call your choice right, good, love, or God, when you choose love, you are choosing to *give*. If you choose fear, you are choosing to *take*. I believe that each and every one of us is either a giver or a taker. I believe God is love.

~~~~~~~

I primarily grew up in a small southern town in North Carolina called Wendell. I do not have any memories of living with both of my parents. When I was fairly young, my mother left my father, taking my brother Ryan and I with her. The story goes that my mother took everything except one fork, one knife, one spoon, one bowl, and one plate. Dad maintains that her leaving came as a complete surprise. However, between his alcoholism and, as my Grandfather describes it, his being a bit of a "hound dog", perhaps he should have seen it coming.

I know that both of my parents loved us dearly, but between battling their personal demons and their issues with each other, they weren't exactly the most effective parents at the time. One day I was forced to ask myself a valuable question: who taught them to be parents? My brother and I became pawns in their war of bitterness. I remember them constantly getting into arguments over the phone. My father would complain about my mother not letting him speak to my brother or me. My mother would constantly remind us that we had a no-good drunk for a father who never paid his child support and therefore must not care very much for his own children.

One weekend my father's side of the family was having a Sunday get-together and he wanted my brother and me to attend. He called my mother every half-hour Friday night through Sunday morning without answer. When my father showed up at the house, I remember my mother becoming a little anxious. She spoke to him through the door, standing firm in her belief that not paying child support meant no visitation. I don't remember everything that transpired, but at one point my mother cracked the door to speak with my father. He forced the door open and pushed his way inside, almost knocking my mother over on the way in. She rushed to the telephone to try and call the police, but my father had already unplugged the phone from the phone jack before she could even dial the nine of 911. As she moved to try and place herself between my father and my brother and me, Dad pinned her against the wall. He never hit her, but he held her firmly against the wall telling us to go and get in his car while mom kept screaming for us to go to my room and lock the door.

I was frozen in place, tears starting to well up in my eyes, but trying the best that I could to hold it together and comfort Ryan as we huddled up in the middle of the hallway. I was just learning basic arithmetic and Ryan couldn't even tie his shoelaces yet, but there we were being asked to make a choice between the two people that we loved most in this world. What would you do? You love both of your parents and you know that they both love you, but no matter which decision you make, you know that it is going to devastate the parent who is not chosen.

I'm not sure why I decided to take Ryan and get in my father's car that day. Maybe it was because we didn't get to see him very often and I missed him. I may just have been scared and wanted the yelling to stop; it may have just been a way to protect my mother. Maybe it was because I had never seen him as angry as he was when he pinned my mother against that wall.

Or maybe I was afraid of what saying no to him might mean for my brother and me. Either way, I grabbed Ryan and we walked outside with my father following behind us. As we backed out of the driveway, I watched my mother's face through the storm door. I was too young to understand the betrayal, but I was old enough to sense disappointment and I could see it in the wet mascara smeared across her face.

~~~~~~~

Both of my parents were takers. They were so focused on themselves, their needs, their desires, and their aspirations that they were completely oblivious to the impacts their selfishness would have in my life and the life of my brother. I have seen the statistics for genetic influence. I've heard the arguments for nature versus nurture, but I hold fast to the Word of God, which warns us clearly about the effects of generational sin:

> *Exodus 34:7: "Maintaining love to thousands, and forgiving wickedness, rebellion and sin. Yet He does not leave the guilty unpunished; he punishes the children and their children for the sin of the parents to the third and fourth generation." (NIV)*

Why is it that kids of alcoholics swear that they will never turn out like their parents, but they do? Why is it that the father that can't control his rage raises a son who can't restrain his anger? Why is it that the mother who suffers from anxiety and depression has a daughter who lives life in fear? Science would argue that these are "learned behaviors," but the Bible is clear how bondage is passed down through the generations.

My mother suffered from anxiety and depression as did her mother. There were feelings of such low self-worth, living largely in guilt. Imagine my surprise when I learned that many of the issues that I had with my mother she also had with hers. It's frustrating to think that despite all the things that my mother went through, she couldn't say that things were going to be different with me and my brother and that she was going to be the one that broke the cycle. After all, it just takes one person to break the bondage, right? As much as I wanted to be different from my mother and my father, it was anxiety and depression that led me onto the overpass that evening with every intention of taking my life.

Eventually, I was freed from the bondage of fear and depression. Friends, let me tell you that it begins with accepting God's grace and mercy.

But do you know what one of the biggest factors in getting down from that bridge was? It was the memory of one of the *givers* from my childhood that helped me to remember that there is goodness and love in this world, something worth living for.

That person was my grandmother. I'm sure that statement might be a little confusing, especially since I just used my grandmother as an example for perpetuating bondage, but she is an even better example of overcoming it and making the choice to become a giver rather than a taker.

I am proud to say that I played a role in her transformation! Nanny was an alcoholic, but the day that I was born was also the last day that she had a drink. I did not know this until years into to my adulthood. Despite all of her issues in raising my mother, it was as if God was giving her a chance to reconcile her pain and regret.

After my parents had separated, Nanny moved in with us. She was nurturing and patient. She was all the things that my mother wasn't ready to be. Unfortunately, the disparity between who she was as a mother and who she had become as a grandmother created even more bitterness and tension in her relationship with her daughter. But oh, what a difference she made in my life!

~~~~~~~

My Nanny was a living illustration that your status as a giver or taker is not static. Ultimately, at any point in someone's life, they are either a giver or a taker. I would also suggest that every

7

single one of us simultaneously plays both roles depending on the dynamics of the relationships in our lives.

You may be a tremendous giver in your marriage and a taker as a parent, a giver as a friend and a taker as a coworker. If you are honest with yourself, I am sure you can think of at least one relationship in which you are a taker. The truth is that givers are very often taken for granted or taken advantage of and in the flesh, it almost becomes necessary to find a relationship that allows you to become the taker. Being a constant giver can be overwhelming; if you are a giver surrounded by *takers*, you know exactly what I'm talking about and you know I am telling the truth. However, if you are a taker, you are probably asking yourself why on earth you would want to be a giver; it sounds exhausting!

The truth is that all those negative words we talked about earlier - wrong, fear, evil, sin - all originate with someone choosing to take. Did you catch that, my friend? It does not matter who you are, color or creed, or where you draw the line between good and evil. Every single act that you consider to be wrong starts with greed and making the decision to put yourself first. Choosing to take is what causes the conflict in our lives and the lives of those around us. For this reason, I want to go back to the burnt-out giver for one second because I'm sure there are some of you who feel like you are trying so hard to give, but you only end up feeling used and exploited.

Once you get burned a few times it's natural to want to protect yourself and build walls. You begin to exhibit a little more caution and a little less trust. You begin to blame others for all the conflict that arises in your life. Blame begins to shift into resentment, resentment becomes bitterness, and then bitterness transforms into anger.

Friend, if you haven't figured it out already, you will reach a point in your life when you look around and there will be no one left to blame. When you look back in contemplation of how and when things went wrong; you will eventually come to the stark realization that the only person you have to blame is yourself.

In regards to your personal journey and to becoming a giver, I can tell you that if you do not have a personal relationship with Jesus Christ, chances are you're somewhere between a frustrated and/or angry giver, even to the point of not giving at all. If you are feeling this way, let me tell you, the conflict you are experiencing in your life is not coming from outside sources and relationships. It is not psychological or philosophical. What you are experiencing is conflict of the heart.

You will not become a complete giver until you completely give yourself to Him. Man is imperfect, born into sin, and incapable of loving or giving completely. So it's no wonder when we try to rely on our capabilities as givers we become tired, anxious, and bitter. But when you have a personal relationship with The Giver, you can cast all of your cares on Him and He will sustain you:

> *Psalm 55:22, "When you grow tired, He will give you strength. When you get anxious, He will give you patience. When you grow bitter or resentful, He will give you peace." [NIV]*

Saint Augustine tells us in *Confessions* that our hearts are restless until they find rest in God. Friend, if you take nothing else from this book, let me tell you there is nothing in this world that will fill the God-shaped hole in your heart. You may find temporary happiness in the pursuit of money, status, success, relationships, and a million other things; however, none of these things will bring you sustainable joy. Nothing is like the joy you will find by surrendering yourself to Jesus Christ and having a personal relationship with Him. You will also find that *you will not* be destroyed when you let loose of any material and worldly things.

~~~~~~~

Conflict! It is an opportunity to make a choice, and we have already established that our choices are what define us.

9

As I mentioned in the Prologue, my perspective on obstacles has changed. When I face a hurdle in my life, I know that God is using it to teach me. He is stretching me, growing me, and drawing me closer to Him.

Now I'm not saying that I look forward to difficulty; nobody wants to go through pain and suffering. I am saying when I recognize new obstacles in my life, I surrender myself to the will and authority of my Father and embrace the opportunity to learn the lesson He would have me learn.

It is my belief that no matter what your personal calling may be, we are all created to love and serve one another as we experience life together and face its many adversities.

Obstacles are not simply something that you go through, around, or over. When you truly confront and overcome an obstacle, it becomes a part of you. It functions as a teaching tool that not only helps you define who you are as an individual, but how you perceive and take action in the world. If the bricks of your obstacles are left in your wake, you will most likely end up tripping over them again later in life. But if you own them and make them yours, then those bricks can be used to lay the foundation for success. Conflict can teach us many things such as patience, trust, resolve, and compassion for others. However, the main building block for success that I want to share with you is *confidence*.

Conflict (Worldview) – The phrase "what doesn't kill you makes you stronger" has become so prevalent in our society that it borders on cliché (thanks, Kelly Clarkson). However, it does ring with some truth. Everyone has experienced and overcome conflict. Often the circumstances and the scale of conflict will change, but the plan of attack is the same and it starts with remembering who you are and where you have come from.

"Let your previous victories give you confidence for your future challenges. " S. Scoggins

There are a million and one studies on how being optimistic and walking in confidence can positively impact your life. Positive thinkers have better relationships socially and in the workplace. They experience a higher rate of success and usually live healthier lives with a longer life expectancy. Confident people worry and complain less, are more trusting, and are generally more content.

Conflict (Faith Perspective) – Paul says in II Corinthians, "Therefore I will boast all the more gladly about my weaknesses, so that Christ's power may rest on me. That is why, for Christ's sake, I delight in weaknesses, in insults, in hardships, in persecutions, in difficulties. For when I am weak, then I am strong" (12:9-10 NIV). God uses obstacles in our lives, not because He wants to see us struggle or suffer, but because adversity allows us to experience His amazing grace and mercy more fully by confronting our weaknesses. Obstacles construct strength in character and confidence not in ourselves, but in God's faithfulness. One of my favorite songs is *Chris Tomlin's, "Whom Shall I Fear".* It's loaded with Biblical truth.

Deuteronomy 31:7-8: "Be strong and courageous...the Lord himself goes before you and will be with you; he will never leave you nor forsake you." [NIV]

"Do not be afraid; do not be discouraged." Life in Christ is not a life of fear, but a life of confidence. Solomon tells us in Proverbs 28:1 that Christians (the righteous) should be as bold as lions. Did you hear that? BOLD AS LIONS! We are told just a bit further in Proverbs 30:30 that a lion is "mighty among beasts, who retreats from nothing" [NIV], "a warrior...which doesn't back down at anything" [CEB], and "deferring to none" [The Message]. And, yet, so many believers still live with anxiety. Brothers and sisters, there is no room in love for fear. Well-formed love banishes fear. Fear is crippling: a fearful life, fear of death, and fear of judgment is a sign of one not yet fully formed in love.

"There is no fear in love. But perfect love drives out fear, because fear has to do with punishment. The one who fears is not made perfect in love."

1 John 4:18

Reflective Notes:

_____

_____

_____

_____

_____

_____

_____

_____

_____

_____

Journey Principle 2: "Growing from Anxiety"

Prayer

Father in Heaven, thank you so much for your grace, power, and mercy. Please deliver me from all things in my life, my relationships, and my actions that bring forth any essence of anxiety! Help me to see that which you have planned for me. Land me sure-footed on sturdy ground and remove that which causes unease in my life or help me to see the purpose behind its design. All of Heaven and Earth is in your hand. In Jesus' name, amen.

Stephen Scoggins

Journey Principle 2:
"Growing from Anxiety"

In the first principle, we discussed fear related to conflict and how choosing fear can affect your status as a giver or taker. In this principle, I want to distinguish the differences between fear and anxiety and how anxiety can become an obstacle in and of itself. I believe that fear and anxiety are similar, but very different things. Fear is a response to a defined and direct danger. For example, if a mugger confronts you with a knife or gun, there is a clear and immediate threat which elicits fear. Anxiety, on the other hand, is very often a reaction to an unclear or an unidentified threat. It has not happened and may never happen, but your mind perceives an object, person, or event as a potential threat. Another and, perhaps, simpler way to look at it is that fear is a reaction to current events and anxiety is directed toward future events.

Think about a time in your life when you were truly afraid. Maybe as a child, there was a time when you encountered a snake in the woods or you got lost or separated from your parents in a shopping mall. I had a bully that lived in my neighborhood when I was growing up that used to terrorize me. He was huge! When he got angry, his eyes turned red, and he grew six inches! Okay, maybe that didn't really happen, but I do know that he was only ten and I am pretty sure he shaved. Anyway, I remember being overwhelmed by fear and panic at what he might do if he got his hands on me. The threat was immediate, and my brain started the biological reaction which creates nervousness and stress. My muscles tightened and my heart began to beat faster and faster. I'm sure that most of you are familiar with the fight or flight theory; it's when we are confronted with what could be a harmful situation or a threat to our survival that we choose either to stand and fight or to run away. Well, when that bully came running after me, my instincts told me to run away and I did. Unfortunately, a few of those times I was caught and received a beating.

There are times when fear is appropriate. I know that I

spent part of the previous principle saying that you shouldn't be afraid, but I want to make a definite distinction between living in fear and the response to a threatening situation. The biological response of fear helps us gain the knowledge of what is and what is not harmful and putting that knowledge into practice is the definition of wisdom. However, there is a glaring difference between the practical application of fear and experiencing anxiety based on the perception of future events that may or not occur.

"Worrying is carrying tomorrow's load with today's strength – carrying two days at once. It is moving into tomorrow ahead of time. Worrying doesn't empty tomorrow of its sorrow; it empties today of its strength." - Corrie Ten Boom

The truth is that we have very little effect on what happens in our lives. The majority of things that happen to us or around us are outside of our control. We very often let the anxiety of future events negatively affect how we live in the present. Life is still about the 90/10 rule: life is 90% the attitude and knowledge used to deal with the situation and only 10% what happens.

~~~~~~~

Did you know that anxiety disorders are the most common mental illness in the United States? Nearly twenty percent of Americans ages eighteen or older suffer from some form of anxiety disorder in a given year[1]. That's one in five Americans.

I don't know about you, but that number seems staggering to me; yet, there are two reasons that this statistic becomes even heavier. First, and most obvious, the statistic only includes ages eighteen and up. Second, the statistic specifically states that it includes anxiety *"disorders"* which means the

---

[1]National Institute of Mental Health

number is a projection of those individuals who have actually been clinically diagnosed. What about the people who haven't sought professional help? What about those whose anxiety may not be debilitating, but still greatly influences their quality of life? Now add the number of kids under the age of eighteen. How many Americans would you guess suffer from anxiety? Twenty-five percent? A third? Half?

Now, I'm not a scientist or a statistician, but it doesn't take more than common sense to see how real this matter has become. In 1980, just over thirty years ago, it was estimated that only between two and four percent of the population experienced anxiety disorder. The number of people struggling with fear and anxiety is growing rapidly and we are not talking about an outbreak. We are talking about an epidemic.[2]

When I was only seven years old, I woke up one morning a little earlier than usual. I yawned. Stretched. I thought about rolling over and going back to sleep, but the smell of bacon had floated from the kitchen, down the hall, and into my bedroom, urging me to wake up and see what else Nanny was cooking. We usually had cereal or something simple for breakfast. Bacon was a treat and it was never cooked alone!

I started down the hall, slowly putting one foot in front of the other on the old, copper-colored carpet. As I approached my mother's bedroom, I began to hear a strange noise. I put my ear to the door and heard what sounded like labored screeching for breathing, but it quickly turned into an all-out gasping for air. I yelled down the hall, "Nanny, Nanny, hurry! It sounds like something is wrong with mommy!"

Nanny moved as quickly as she could and knocked on the door. There was no answer. She knocked harder and screamed my mother's name. Still no answer, but the wheezing became more concentrated, deeper, and longer. Nanny began to pound on the door, arms and feet, hitting and kicking with all the strength her frail frame could afford. I saw the terror in her

[2] Resource Allan V. Horwitz is Board of Governors Professor of Sociology at Rutgers University. He is the author of numerous articles and books on various aspects of the sociology of mental illness, including "The Social Control of Mental Illness," "Creating Mental Illness" and "The Loss of Sadness" with Jerome C. Wakefield.

eyes intensify as she realized that there was nothing she could do to open the door and reach her daughter. Nanny was maybe 130lbs soak and wet and to break the door down was not an option. These doors were old school-constructed and solid wood.

A few months earlier, I had figured out that I could pick the lock to my mother's room with one of my ninja stars that were given to me as a gift. I developed a fascination with martial arts and especially ninjas that was likely due to constantly being bullied and my need to feel protected. I originally started playing with the locks so that I could sneak in and look at Christmas presents. Of course, I did not want Nanny or my mother to know what I had done or could do - so I hesitated, but as I watched my grandmother panic, I knew what I had to do.

"I can open that door," I said shamefully while staring at the floor. "What did you say, honey?" she asked in disbelief.

"I can open that door, Nanny," I said once more. Hope awakened in her eyes. "Do whatever you need to do, Stephen," she said in a panic.

I sprinted to my room and back, star in hand, and with a quick shake and turn the door lock popped. Nanny seemed like she was through the door before I even unlocked it. She ran to my mother who was spread across her bed. Nanny kept screaming her name as she picked my mother's head up and cradled it in her arms. There was no lucid response, only shortened panting. Water dripped down the nightstand from an overturned glass onto a damp spot on the floor that was sprinkled with the few pills Mother had not taken and an empty medication bottle. The paramedics showed up shortly thereafter and began doing what seemed to be CPR. They loaded her in the ambulance and it seemed like literal years before I would see my mother again.

~~~~~~~

Deception is the enemy's strongest weapon, but there are many tools that he will use in order to deceive. He will use fear and anxiety to play on your insecurities, crafting concern for judgment from others and fashioning feelings of worthlessness and insignificance.

If he hasn't already flooded you with guilt for what you have done in the past, then he will whisper in your ear that you are not strong enough to handle the uncertain road before you. Your concerns that once seemed like minor distractions will begin to consume you. Some say a little of this is hereditary, but I believe it to be one generation not trained to teach the next how to deal with overwhelming pain and hurt in life. This is why I believe the cycle to continue through family bloodlines. There are very few families who can deal with their personal struggle let alone teach another how to deal with theirs.

These thoughts and emotions will start to affect work, friendships, and family. Soon you won't only be afraid of the future, but you will become so frightened of the results of your immediate decisions that you will choose inaction instead of the possibility of failure. Without action, your life will begin to become void of the positive interactions and experiences that give life meaning and you may begin to wonder if life is really worth living at all.

My Mother reached a point where fear and anxiety consumed her so much that she decided to take her life. I am thankful that at the time of writing this book she is still present and growing in her walk. I am not sure how exactly, but the doctors waiting in the ER seemed to have just enough time to pump the pills from her stomach. She got a second chance at life.

Now, in a principle about anxiety you may think that my mother's fear is the obvious discussion point. It is a good illustration of the effects of fear, but the part of the story that I still often think about was my anxiety.

At such a young age, it's difficult to weigh the repercussions of one's actions or inactions. I knew that I could get that door open, but I was so worried about getting in trouble for peeking at my Christmas presents that I literally froze in place, not giving a thought as to what was going on outside of my own circumstances.

I believe that God is sovereign and that He had plans for

my mother beyond that day whether I took action or not. However, for those of you who do not share my faith, what if my hesitation was the difference in the paramedics arriving in time? What if my inaction would have been the difference in my mother's survival?

Now, I do not operate in *"what ifs"*. I operate in trust! Whether you believe in God or not, you must recognize the fact that your fears and anxieties will affect not only your life, but also the lives of those around you. Those same anxieties could be the very thing holding you back from a life-giving journey of your own.

Have you ever met someone who is a worst-case-scenario person? Or maybe you have a friend or a coworker who seems to exist in the world of *"what ifs"*. Does it seem like their worry and stress is contagious? It's almost like their negativity acts like a virus, feeding and multiplying until any joy that may have existed is gone. We talked in Principle One about how fear can cause you to be a taker. Well, living with fear and anxiety will not only take from your life, but it will steal from those around you and, eventually, push people away.

Fear will seize happiness, peace, and joy. It will rob you of the ability to make good decisions and to experience life fully. Most importantly, living in fear will not allow you to love or to be loved completely. You give up being vulnerable and real in your relationships. Consequently, no real connection is made and eventually the luster is washed away due to a lack of connection.

~~~~~~~

We have already looked at how the obstacle of conflict is converted into the building block of confidence.

Confidence is a major ingredient in overcoming fear and anxiety, but confidence is a byproduct of trust and faith.

You might be saying that trust and faith are the same things and, according to the thesaurus, you would be correct. Let's look at both trust and faith. I want to be able to provide both believers and nonbelievers with a path for action and direction. I will use *trust* as the building block for the worldview and *faith* as the building block for the faith perspective. Of course, you know which path I recommend! My grandfather, who led me to Christ, used to tell me "there was no condemnation in God."

Here are five action steps for overcoming fear and learning to T.R.U.S.T.

1. ***Take action!*** Do not let fear freeze you. Learn to recognize, analyze, and take action toward overcoming your fears and anxieties. Taking action builds confidence! One helpful way to accomplish this is to use a calendar. Pick a date and time to pull the trigger on a decision. This is a decision that keeps you moving forward. I first heard of this concept in 2011 while attending "EntreLeadership" for the first time. Dave Ramsey himself said, "There is no such thing as a spineless leader. All real leaders must know when to pull the trigger, even if it is gently."

2. ***Release!*** Practice letting go of things beyond your control. I know this is a hard one, but I promise that it gets easier with practice. You will be amazed at how much time it frees up so you can focus on the things that you can change. Do not let worrying about tomorrow affect what you can affect today. Mathew 6:34 *"Therefore do not worry about tomorrow, for tomorrow will worry about itself. Each day has enough trouble of its own."* *[NIV]*

3. ***Unarm yourself!*** I think I could write an entire book on this topic alone. Criss Jami summed it up best when he said, "To share your weakness is to make yourself vulnerable; to make yourself vulnerable is to show your

strength." Break down your defensive walls and become vulnerable. It is worth the risk!

4. **_Serve!_** Serving builds trust. When you serve, not only will you learn more about your own potential, but you will also awaken the potential of those around you, and that, my friend, is Proverbs 27:17, my personal life verse and the reason for this book: *"As iron sharpens iron so should one sharpen another."* *[NIV]*

5. **_Talk!_** Open healthy lines of communication and share your heart. Your transparency will motivate others to be open as well and trust will grow. Your relationships will deepen. The only words of caution are this: *It's important to share things with someone who is an encourager, not a detractor.* It has worked best for me to get around the heat. For me, this means finding someone I trust to lead me where I want to go because they have already been there and overcame. Once you have found this solid accountability partner, open up! It's very important to make sure the person you are following is in front of you and not some missionary friendship where two hurt people are trying to fix each other. Healing is too important to us as a people.

FAITH (Faith Perspective) – How many of you have ever taken an art class in middle school or high school? Somewhere in the lesson on the color wheel you learn that black is not a color, but rather it is the absence of light. Scientists will also tell you that there is no such thing as cold, only the absence of heat. Likewise, I believe that fear is nothing more than the absence of faith. On a snowy day, there is nothing better than sitting in front of the fireplace and wrapping up in a warm blanket to escape the cold. Escaping fear is as easy as blanketing yourself in the warmth and comfort of faith.

I have personally found my greatest faith and peace in

Jesus Christ. This book is all about the journey, and you, the reader, will need to make your own decision. Paul tells us in Ephesians 2:8, "For it is by grace you have been saved, through faith—and this not from yourselves, it is the gift of God." [NIV]
Faith is not something that we can attain on our own. It is a gift freely given. However, faith cannot mature without adversity. Life will present obstacles, but each obstacle is an opportunity to grow closer to God and to cultivate a more resilient faith. When we struggle and walk on faith it helps us to see that, much like the parable of the five talents in the Bible, the more faithful we are, the more our faith is increased over time. The important thing to remember is that God's mercies are new for us each and every day!

Relying on God has to begin again every day as if it had never been done. Each day becomes a newer improved building block. Jesus was a carpenter, right? I trust that Jesus is there for us and enough for us in times of crisis. Jesus said, "...surely I am with you always, to the very end of the age." *[Matthew 28:20, NIV]*

Here are five action steps for overcoming fear and maintaining F.A.I.T.H.

1. ***Fix your eyes!*** "Fix your eyes on Jesus, the author and perfector of faith" *[Hebrews 12:2, NIV]*. Jesus is our greatest illustration of suffering! Though sinless, He chose to take on the weight of our sin and, in faithfulness for His Father's plan, gave His life so that we might experience joy.

2. ***Ask!*** Prayer is one of the ways that we exhibit faith. God uses our obstacles to draw us closer to Him, so if you do not understand or cannot see what He is trying to teach you, go to Him. He will be your supply. He will provide for you richly and abundantly. Ask Him for strength, patience, perseverance, comfort and, most importantly, ask Him to reveal Himself to you. Seek His plan and

25

purpose for your life! "Do not be anxious about anything, but in every situation, by prayer and petition, with thanksgiving, present your requests to God. And the peace of God, which transcends all understanding, will guard your hearts and your minds in Christ Jesus." *[Philippians 4:6-7, NIV]*

3. ***Incorporate!*** Sometimes when we seek God's will, we don't like the answer that He gives us. It is sometimes easy for us to ignore God's instruction and seek our own will, but how foolish would it be to hear from God and not incorporate His instruction in your life? Faith is not only believing in God's provision, but trusting Him and aligning your heart with His will and purpose for your life.

4. ***Track!*** C.S. Lewis said in *The Screwtape Letters* that life is "a series of troughs and peaks." Your spiritual life will experience highs and lows, but I have found that one of the best ways to combat the lows is to remind yourself of the highs. Keep a prayer journal and track the ways that God is moving and working in your life. Remember His faithfulness and the wonders and miracles He has done.

5. ***Honor one another!*** Faith is meant to be shared! It's that simple, friend. Sometimes we get caught up in our own issues, but we should never forget the power of our testimony and our responsibility of witnessing to those around us. God will use your faith as a tool to encourage others. "...let your light shine before men, that they may see your good deeds and praise your Father in heaven." *[Matthew 5:16, NIV]*

"These are truths which can prepare us to respond when crisis and fear come into our lives."

C.S. Lewis

Reflective Notes:

_____

_____

_____

_____

_____

_____

_____

_____

_____

_____

Journey Principle 3: "Isolation is a TRAP!"

Prayer

Oh, Heavenly Father, please install a hedge of protection over me and give your angels charge of me. Keeping me from the evil one; I know he wants to isolate me in aloneness or in unhealthy relationships. Father, please guide me towards life-giving relationships, relationships that are full of your love, mercy, and grace. Create in me a life-giving spirit so I may guide others to you and your purpose for them. In Jesus' name, amen.

Stephen Scoggins

Journey Principle 3:
"Isolation is a TRAP!"

John Donne tells us in *Meditation XVII* that "no man is an island, entire of itself," and I believe that most people would agree. There are definitely some of us that are more independent than others, but, as I have already stated, I think that most people recognize the importance of relationships. Humans desire contact, connection, and support from one another. My faith states that relationships are quite literally the reason we were created: to love and to be loved. Even atheists such as Karl Marx and Emile Durkheim studied the damaging effects that isolation and alienation can have in a person's life. Quite simply, a support system is necessary to help cope with the everyday stresses of life.

Without sympathy, empathy, encouragement, and validation, stress begins to be internalized and can lead to a decline in both physical and mental health. However, when the right support system is in place and a person knows that they are not going to have to confront life's obstacles on their own, no problem seems too big.

In 2006, the American Sociological Review published a study that showed that from 1985 to 2004, "the number of people saying there is no-one with whom they discuss important matters nearly tripled" to close to 25% of Americans. An additional 20% admitted to having only one such relationship.

I'm no math wizard, but those statistics show that nearly half of the U.S. population has one or no one with whom they share the significant matters of their life. I don't know about you, but that sounds like a country wrestling with loneliness, right? Loneliness can have a number of impacts on both the body and the mind!

I really enjoy Pastor Matt Fry's personal and church mission. His vision statement reads, "Real Hope for Real People in a Real World". He calls this "Doing life together." It seems that both he and his congregation have figured out the secret to healthy well-being and that is quality relationships. Quality

31

relationships start with God.

It is very important to realize that a quality person can make a quality impact on everyone they know and meet.

John Cacioppo (the co-author of *Loneliness Human Nature and the Need for Social Connection*) identified that loneliness and isolation can lead to increased stress levels, cardiovascular disease, diminishing memory, the inability to learn, an increase in bad decision making, drug abuse, alcoholism, altered brain function, the progression of Alzheimer's disease, antisocial behavior, depression and even suicide.

As if that list wasn't long enough, Cacioppo adds that lonely people also exercise less, have poor dietary practices, have less efficient sleep, and experience more daytime fatigue, all factors that can lead to premature aging and death. To top it off, loneliness, fear and anxiety can be contagious!

Now, that was a lot of science and I hate to throw more at you, but if you are a visual person like me, sometimes a simple illustration is a more useful teaching tool. Here is an example: do you remember the Clydesdale horses from the Budweiser commercials? Great! Now picture one horse pulling a large amount of weight. You see, they have tested these horses and in amazement they found the following: one Clydesdale can pull six tons of weight. Now that sounds like a lot and for you and I it would be, but when he is joined to his partner the two horses can pull thirty-six tons. Did you catch that? That is more than double the weight and is only possible with quality companionship.

In addition, studies show that when both teamwork and accountability are introduced, morale increases as well as the potential workload. Now imagine a third, fourth or a fifth horse. (Next time you get stuck on a project, think Clydesdale.)

The same concept can be applied to emotional and spiritual weight. You can try to carry the weight by yourself, but it's so much easier when you have the right support group to help you shoulder the load. It's simple and intuitive, but statistics show that loneliness and isolation continue to grow.

I'm sure that there are a number of theories as to why

isolation is escalating in our country, but in my mind there are two main contributors: first, our ever-growing desire for individualism; second, the rapid increase in technology.

Now let me be clear in stating, I do not believe that individualism is necessarily a bad thing, but anything in excess can be harmful. King David tells us:

> "For you created my inmost being; you knit me together in my mother's womb. I praise you because I am fearfully and wonderfully made; your works are wonderful, I know that full well." *[Psalms 139:13-14, NIV]*

We are uniquely and beautifully crafted with our own individual talents and skills. God created us with a special plan and purpose and we should want to explore and fulfill our potential. The question is this: are you seeking God's plan for your life or are you seeking your own selfish desires?

I believe that we live in a "me" society that champions material wealth, and has made an idol of success by placing the self above all. Unfortunately, the result has been a culture of swelling discontent, jealousy and resentment. That's individualism; that is the "me" society.

True individualism promotes both the individual and the group, but if it pushes away or harms those around you, then it is being practiced in an unhealthy way that will most likely lead to loneliness and isolation.

One of our most valuable teaching tools is this principle from the late and truly great Zig Ziglar:

> "You don't build a business --you build people-- and then people build the business."

Now, when we apply that to a real world scenario in relationships, we see this manifesting in areas around us. Here is another shared principle that requires a little meditation and thought:

"Hurt People – Hurt People!"

33

Please think about that for a moment. With this principle, then conversely this next statement would be true as well.

"Healed People - Heal People!"

I was at dinner one evening and at the table behind me was what looked like an example of the perfect American family. The mother and father were probably in their late thirties or early forties. Dad looked like he played an important role somewhere in Corporate America and Mom was in her gym gear, maybe heading to spin class or yoga after dinner. The daughter, who was probably fifteen or sixteen, had on her high school cheerleading uniform and little Brother, probably twelve, was decked out in his soccer gear. What a good looking family they were except for one thing: the father was either talking on his phone or checking emails, the son was only taking bites of dinner in between levels of his video game, the daughter was back and forth between texting and social media, and the mother sat there quietly, her foot nervously bouncing on the floor, with a look on her face that said she just wanted to get out of there and get to the gym. During the course of the dinner, each one of them probably said *more* to the server than they did to each other.

For someone who didn't grow up in the strongest family atmosphere and who is still waiting on God's promise to start my own family, it made me so sad to watch them not take advantage of their time together. I wept inside at the loss they do not understand. I am a man who cannot have biological children of my own and to watch as others seem to squander the gift desperately stings my soul.

Family dinners have turned into TV dinners. Friendship has turned into Facebook. Relationships and fellowships are suffering. People are walking around with their head in the cloud (yes, pun intended). And for all this time spent in the virtual world, we sure are starting to see some very real and tangible walls being built between us.

Did you know that according to Pew Research Center the average Facebook user has 338 friends? True. Then we have the statistic mentioned earlier that shows that most people in America have one or less person with whom they can discuss the important things in life. Now, I am not a sociologist, psychologist, or psychiatrist and I am not going to pretend that I am smart enough to come up with a solution to the problem. However, it is obvious to me that a problem exists and I do not believe it is a coincidence that as technology has exponentially advanced that our concepts of relationship and fellowship have exponentially decayed.

Lastly, I want to recognize the role that fear and anxiety play in isolation. I didn't list it as a contributor before because I just used an entire principle discussing its negative effects, but fear of judgment has an obvious impact on letting others get close to you. More than that, letting others in also opens us up to accountability. For a country that cherishes individualism and its privacy alike, this presents risk and responsibilities that many people are unwilling or afraid to take.

~~~~~~~

The first step in developing a proper support team has nothing to do with choosing the right friends. Before you can trust the opinions and feedback from those closest to you, you must first know yourself! Relationships are built on trust and as we explored in the last principle, trust begins with you.

Knowing yourself is not as simple as stating a social meme, a socially excepted belief system, or fundamental moral ethics. It means acting in accordance with *your* beliefs, not just occasionally, but consistently.

Integrity is being the same person when no one else is looking.

"Integrity is doing the right thing, even when no one is watching." C.S. Lewis

While trust is widely considered the most important element in successful relationships, the reason that we give someone trust is because they display consistency.

"We are what we repeatedly do. Excellence, then, is not an act, but a habit."

Aristotle

In every single one of your relationships (social or professional), your character and reputation will be judged by the things that you consistently do. Today, the term that I believe is most comparable with Aristotle's definition of excellence is integrity.

I would argue that integrity is the single driving factor in whether or not a business will be successful. It's how companies choose employees and, in turn, how customers choose companies. At one of my businesses, Custom Home Exteriors (CHE), we use the words "integrity" and "excellence" in our mission statement because we know that it is imperative that we don't just sell a product or service, but that we share a vision built on reputation. That's how we build business relationships and, call me crazy, but isn't that a great way to build personal relationships as well? I don't want friends who are only there because of what I can do for them. I want friends who respect and trust my vision and my purpose, and vice-versa.

Without integrity or consistency of character, your relationships will be short-lived. You might argue that true friendship can endure any hardship, but I contend that any relationship that demonstrates that level of strength was built on a firm foundation of character and some level of shared ethical standards.

Inconsistency or deviation from the original bond, without integrity, is usually when conflict arises in a relationship. In addition, if you do not have a solid grasp on who you are and what you stand for, then you may end up being taken advantage of!

I mentioned in Principle One how givers can sometimes be exploited in their giving. I have found that people who lack a strong sense of personal identity are usually trying so hard to find a place to fit in that they become easily manipulated. Knowing yourself can help you draw the line between giving and exploitation. However, I can tell you that the line between giving and exploitation changes as your heart is conditioned to give.

As a Christian, I continuously seek out ways in which to give and serve because I know that I am the vessel that demonstrates God's character to the world. Friend, my God, is a giver! Even though there are times when I know that someone may be trying to take advantage of me, my heart can remain at peace and hold no resentment because sharing God's mercy and grace has become so important in my life.

I'm sure that if I asked you what the most important building block in a relationship was, you would probably say love and you would be right. It's the obvious and correct answer, but love itself displays many different characteristics. If you have ever attended a wedding then, you have probably heard 1 Corinthians 13:4-7 which says that:

> "Love is patient, love is kind. It does not envy, it does not boast, it is not proud, it does not dishonor others, it is not self-seeking, it is not easily angered, it keeps no record of wrongs. Love does not delight in evil but rejoices with the truth. It always protects, always trusts, always hopes, and always perseveres." *[NIV]*

This is the description of the perfect love of God. (On a side note to the men out there, please study this verse because it tells you exactly how God expects you to love your wives). The amazing thing about this verse is that it's not only describing *how* God loves us, but it is describing *who* He is. It's not something that He turns on or off depending on the person or the circumstance; it's His character, unwavering, unconditional, and unstoppable! Isn't that a marvelous thing to even contemplate? God does not change. He is "the same yesterday, today, and forever." *[Hebrews 13:8, NIV].*)

Even though man was created in God's image, we are not exactly like Him. We were created in his image for communion with Him. We were not created to replace Him. Is it not true that all too often we like to play the Divine Creator in our life, finding all too quickly that we have been lead into sin? We do this by our arrogance and believing we are in total control.

The fact is that every man has sinned and fallen short of the glory of God and while consistency of character is something that we should aim for, there will be times that we miss the mark. We are only human. It's what we do. However, because we exist in inconsistency, we should try to practice forgiveness consistently!

In my humble opinion, because of man's imperfect state, forgiveness is the most important aspect of our relationships. Forgiveness is the correct response when love fails. Just to put that in perspective, look back at the Corinthians verse; if love is impatient, forgive; if it is unkind, forgive; if love envies, boasts, or is proud...forgive!

I'm sure you see the picture that I am trying to paint for you mentally. So I won't continue with the entire verse, but while there are obviously other keys to having successful relationships, I do believe that forgiveness inspired by love may just be the most important.

Developing your team – The building block for Principle Three is family. This term is not limited to actual blood bonds, but also implies friends, mentors, etc. It is essential that you develop these types of relationships in your life and here is why: in Genesis 2:18, God says:

> "It is not good for man to be alone. I will make a helper suitable for him." [NIV]

We were created for relationship, to interact with one another and to help each other. Now for those of you who may not be familiar with this reference, I think that it is very important to know that God declared the significance of fellowship before Adam and Eve chose to eat from the tree of the knowledge of good and evil. Think about this for a moment: if companionship was vital before sin entered the world, how much more important does it become after the fall of man? The fact is that we need each other. We need to serve and encourage each other as we face life's obstacles. We need to help each other avoid temptation. We need to share in each other's joy. We need to use our experience and wisdom to help teach and lead others. We need to show each other mercy and grace in love.

Surround yourself with people that challenge you, facilitate growth in you and can help you in realizing and achieving your full potential. Proverbs 27:17:

"As iron sharpens iron, so one man sharpens another." [NIV]

Yes, I know I have already mentioned it before, but it is the verse that truly speaks to my heart every day of my life and it bears repeating. When you develop sincere relationships where trust can foster honest and open discussion, then our unique differences of thoughts and ideas can help hone and sharpen one another. It is through opposing viewpoints that we may glean truth.

The second aspect of "iron sharpening iron" is accountability. Accountability presents a challenge, a responsibility that many people are either unwilling or too afraid to take. However, the truth is that there may not be anything more important to individual development than accountability.

Finally, not only do we desire and seek fellowship, but our coming together serves a greater purpose. Psalm 131:1 says:

"How good and pleasant it is when brothers live together in unity." [NIV]

You know that I believe the greater purpose is building the Kingdom of God, but even if you are not a person of faith, you cannot argue that unity doesn't have practical applications in your family, in your friendships, and in your workplace. In truth, when we unite in purpose and in "action", amazing things are accomplished.

> Whoever isolates himself seeks his own desire;
> he breaks out against all sound judgment.
>
> Proverbs 18:1 (ESV)

But seek ye first the kingdom of God, and his righteousness; and all these things shall be added unto you.

Matthew 6:33

Reflective Notes:

_____

_____

_____

_____

_____

_____

_____

_____

_____

Journey Principle 4: "Addiction vs. Sanctification"

Prayer

My Father who is in Heaven, holy is your name. Please show me the areas in my life that take me away from you and the addictions that are in front of my relationship with you. Please help me break from them; utterly and completely without changing one addiction for another. Help me see your purpose and plan for my life. And if I must share in something, let it be in you. You are the Alpha and the Omega, the Beginning and the End. Let me not have any other gods before you. In Jesus' name, amen.

Stephen Scoggins

Journey Principle 4:
"Addiction vs. Sanctification"

Have you ever heard the phrase, *"You can change a cucumber into a pickle, but you can never turn a pickle back into a cucumber?"* It's an illustration used in many recovery programs to show how addictions are a life-long battle. This concept of "once an addict, always an addict" explains that while on the road to recovery you will experience improvement and things will start to get better, essentially you will never heal. As someone who is results driven, that phrase just didn't work for me. It's like asking someone for directions to a place that you have never been and they draw you a circle. *(Oh, so I just keep veering to the right and then I stop where?)*. It just doesn't make sense.

However, the more I began to think about it, I realized that addiction is nothing more than a term for the repetition of sin and struggle. Addiction is defined as being controlled by or enslaved to something (or some practice) emotionally and/or physically. The sin struggle is also often referred to as enslavement or bondage. So, "once an addict, always an addict" began to make sense for me because even though I have been saved by the blood of Jesus Christ, I am still a sinner. I still experience temptations and have the potential to sin, just as an addict has the temptation and potential to relapse.

You may not be addicted to drugs or to alcohol, but there is something in your life that controls you. There is something that is the object of your focus, your energy, your time, and/or your finances. In that light, every single one of us is an addict because each and every one of us is a sinner.

When we typically think about addiction, we think of things like drugs, alcohol, or pornography, but sin can come in all shapes and sizes. (Here in the south, that would get an Amen!)

If addiction is the repetition of sin, then there are just as many possibilities for addictions as there are sins. Perhaps it is food or an eating disorder. Maybe it's shopping, spending, gambling, video games, television, social media, work, cigarettes, or coffee (I'm an energy drink man myself). It could be something a little more abstract as the need to have control, lying, success, respect, approval, negativity, or even love.

Perhaps you are reading right now and you are saying, *'Stephen, there are things in my life that I enjoy doing, perhaps on a regular basis, but I wouldn't say that I am addicted.'* I pray that you are correct, but I believe that the majority of people can find at least one addiction in their life if they look hard enough. Furthermore, I would argue that most of us wouldn't even need to look very hard. It may be big or small. It may be obvious or it might be hiding in plain sight, but something is there.

What gives you comfort? What makes you sad or angry? Where does your anxiety and fear originate? How do you spend your money? If the answers to these questions in any way prohibit you from becoming your authentic self, Then they are an addiction and even though you might not yet recognize how they are having a negative effect on you physically and emotionally. I am asking you to ask yourself the above questions. If you answer yes, then there is an addiction happening in your life.

Often in the faith perspective we can attach these addictions to idolatry. Idolatry is the love or worship of anything other than God himself. We have struggles with the balance of enjoying a blessing from God and turning that same blessing into the curse of idolatry. Idolization will bring you pain and causes removal of it from your life. God will not share His glory with any object of affection. This includes a person, a drink, a cigarette, a golden image, etc. You get the picture.

The cool thing that I have learned during my journey is this: God will use all those things that you or evil use to destroy you to create in you His purpose. These struggles bring humbleness to the proud and arrogant. Please keep in mind I am saying this from personal experience. So just in case you are in a battle right now, and feel like the world might be crashing in on you, all you need to know is that if you let God be God and you give way to His purpose for your life, then your trouble, your anguish, your pain will become what Eric Thomas calls "The Prize". Eric Thomas, like me, was once struggling with homelessness amongst other things for his life. Lo and behold God stepped in and now he is one of the most inspiring and powerful speakers for changing what I like to call "The Mental Switch." I will talk more about that later. Eric says a very true statement:

> "Your pain if you let it, will become part of your purpose and prize."

When I was in my early twenties, and when I say *early* I mean twenty, maybe twenty-one, I went with my father one afternoon to eat lunch at Murray's Barbeque in Raleigh, North Carolina.[3]

We had the cutest waitress, and I must admit that there was an instant attraction. I went to eat there a handful of times until I found out that she was only seventeen years old. I had thought that she was in college and was just working a summer job because she was always wearing North Carolina Tar Heel's gear. When I found out that she was a few years younger than me, I decided not to pursue a relationship. She was, however, very persistent. She kept setting up times for a group of our friends to hang out. After a month, I eventually gave in and I let the attraction take hold of me.

Our relationship was extremely physical. I found out later in life, after reading Gary Chapman's "*The 5 Love Languages*", that my primary languages are physical touch and words of affirmation. She was an abundant supply of both. But as with most relationships that begin in lust, the initial attraction began to lose its shine and she became unfaithful. You would think that would be enough to end the relationship, but not only was I addicted to the physicality, my broken childhood had created a need in me to fix things and I became addicted to the idea of saving her. She was addicted to the excitement and attention of new sexual encounters, but she also loved the comfort and reliability that I provided for her both physically

---

[3]*Note to reader: I know a lot of places claim to have the best barbeque, but Eastern North Carolina vinegar-based barbeque is by far THE best barbeque in the world!* Unfortunately, after the passing of the owner it has since closed down.

and financially. Ours was the very definition of a toxic relationship. I have seen many of my friends in very similar relationships, so I know this is a big issue. This is my newest guiding principle as taught by Pastor Matt Fry at C3 church in Clayton, N.C.:

"A true love, a true relationship leaves one feeling full and encouraged, and will have a true intimacy. This intimacy is cultivated over hours, days, weeks and even months of vulnerable communication. This intimacy does not have a physical connection at its core".

I have found it far easier to build a quality relationship taking sex off the table entirely. Yes, I know to most readers it will seem a bit extreme. As one who used to put a great deal of influence in that area, I can honestly say that the purity of one's relationships seems to directly impact the successful growth, communication, and vulnerability that is required to build a relationship that is fruitful and long lasting. The other thing that can make relationships joyful and full of love is to have the vertical one fixed first. I have learned that putting God first breeds success in all areas of my life.

I would hear rumors of some of the guys that she was seeing. While I would initially be angry, my desire to please her and make her happy resulted in trying to change myself in order to become the person that I thought that she desired.

~~~~~~~

I went out and got a couple of tattoos and bought some gold jewelry trying to take on the "bad boy" image that I thought she hungered for, but things didn't change. One day I let her borrow my Camaro and the tires got slashed and the car got keyed. That should have been another clear sign that she was in some kind of trouble. Instead of trying to get to the bottom of why it happened, I just gave her my credit card to go and get new tires. Guess what? I never saw that credit card again. I did however see the thousands of dollars of debt that followed. That one decision took four years of working like a maniac to pay off.

In retrospect, it's easy to see how young, naïve, and foolish I was. There are some of you who may be wondering how I ever let things reach the point that they did. That is exactly how addiction works. It clouds your mind, impairs your judgment, and decreases self-control while increasing impulsiveness. You live in a state of denial, telling yourself that everything is going to be okay. The biggest lie is this: "I have it all under control". In reality, we are racing to drive off a cliff. You become so preoccupied with the addiction that you don't even notice the downward spiral until your face hits the floor or the car is flying over a cliff with a sure fiery burst to come.

One night we got into a huge argument. The cheating, the car, the use of my credit card, the disregard for my feelings, and the total exploitation of me financially, physically, and emotionally had come to a head. I don't remember what it was exactly that she said, but I do remember raising my hand. I wanted to strike out, but in an instant many feelings hit me all at once. The vision of my father breaking into my mother's house and pinning her against the wall came crashing into my mind and my hand dropped to my side.

I never hit her, but I knew that it was time to go. I finally began to see what the addiction had turned me into, and I felt broken, tired and afraid. Unfortunately, it was still some time before I would make my way back towards healing, and it ended in a very dark place in life. It also ended up beside a litter box, but more about that later!

~~~~~~~

What is it that we are looking for when addiction creeps into our lives? Are we simply looking to have a good time to try to add a little excitement to our lives? Is it to take away the pain, both physically and emotionally? Are we looking for answers, comfort, or perhaps to satisfy our most basic needs? Is it how we cope with conflict, anxiety, or isolation? Addictions and the issues that they attempt to pacify are different for every person.

I think that they all have the same origin. I gave you the Augustine quote in Journey Principle one that says "Man's heart remains restless until it finds rests in God," and I believe it to be profoundly true. We live in a society that loves to treat the symptom and not the disease, but the sin in our life has but one cure: Jesus. There are so many things that we use to try and fill that God-shaped hole in our heart. We experience temporary joy, comfort, or satisfaction, but it always fades leaving us feeling just as broken, just as tired, and just as afraid as we did before.

So far in this book I have given action steps for both the believer and the nonbeliever and I will continue to do so in this Journey Principle and some of the principles to follow. I am doing it this way because I realize we are all on our personal journey. I am bound to tell the truth, and as the old adage goes, "The truth will set you free".

As I have defined addiction as the repetition of sin and even mentioned how it could be a form of idolatry, I believe that this is the place to stop and make a very clear distinction: *you can* overcome the sin and the addictions in your life.

You can break the cycle of doing/using. You can heal the wounds both in your heart and in the hearts of your friends and families and find forgiveness. You can renovate your life from brokenness and disrepair to one of strength and purpose. You can achieve every single one of these things. While you may have made amazing efforts to overcome the brokenness, and you have lived a good life with remarkable accomplishments and positive impacts, on that day it will not have been enough. You see, no matter how much effort you put in, no matter what you have overcome, no matter how good or honest or generous or kind or loving you have been, without the reconciliation of your sin which only comes through the grace and mercy of Jesus Christ, your life will be lost. You can experience transformation, but without sanctification there is no victory.

Transformation (Worldview) – When you are fully immersed in addiction, recovery can seem a million miles away. However, it is possible for you to transform your life from one of dependency to one of freedom. I promise you that no matter how bad things appear to be, there is always hope. The 12-step program is used in numerous programs around the world and has helped millions of addicts on their road to recovery.

The 12 Steps[4]

1. **Admit** that you are powerless over addiction and that your life has become unmanageable.
2. **Believe** that a power greater than yourself can restore you to sanity.
3. **Make the decision** to turn your will and life over to the care of God as you understand God.
4. **Take an inventory** of who you are inside and out and whose you are. (The world or the Father's.)
5. **Admit to God**, to yourself and to another human being the exact nature of your wrongs.
6. **Be entirely ready** to have God remove all these defects of character.
7. **Humbly ask God** to remove your shortcomings.
8. **Make a list** of the persons you have wronged and make amends to them all.
9. **Make direct amends** to such people wherever possible, except when to do so would injure them or others.
10. **Continue** to take personal inventory and when you are wrong admit it promptly.
11. **Seek** through prayer and meditation to improve your conscious contact with God as you understand God. Praying only for knowledge of God's will for you and the power to carry it out.
12. **Share the news** of having had a spiritual awakening as the

---

4 Copyright 1952, 1953, 1981 by Alcoholics Anonymous Publishing (now known as Alcoholics Anonymous World Services, Inc.)

result of these steps. Try to carry this message to other addicts and to practice these principles in all your affairs.

Sanctification and Consecration (Faith Perspective) - You can experience transformation, but without sanctification there is no true victory. We are born into sin and while sins and addictions can be overcome, we are still sinners. We can only find atonement through the blood of Jesus Christ who took on the sin of the world and died in our place that we might have everlasting life. When you accept Christ as your personal Lord and Savior, your sins are washed away, and you are made clean. This process is called sanctification which comes from the Hebrew word *qâdâsh*, meaning to make holy, to purify or to prepare. The amazing thing about being made clean through Christ is that it is permanent! In Hebrews, Paul tells us "...we have been made holy through the sacrifice of the body of Jesus Christ once and for all." [Hebrews 10:10, NIV]

Not just for a little while, not as long as we strictly follow the commandments, not as long as we do good works, but forever. 2 Corinthians tells us that in Christ we are a new creation. So there is a transformation that takes place. Not only has the old been replaced with the new, but we are now reconciled to God through Christ.

There is a symbolic representation of this process in Exodus when God instructs Moses to anoint and ordain his brother Aaron and his sons. Anointing and ordination, or sanctification and consecration, was one of the ways (along with some pretty cool threads!) that they distinguished the priests of Israel. In that day, the priests were the only ones who could obtain direct supervision from God for His people. They alone were allowed to enter the Holy of Holies, the inner sanctum where God's earthly presence dwelled and seek atonement for the sins of Israel. They literally tied a rope to the priest's ankle to pull his body from the room in case he died in God's presence. But when Christ gave His life for the sins of man and "gave up His Spirit. At that moment, the curtain of the temple was torn in two from top to bottom. The earth shook, and the rocks split" (Matthew 27:50-51,NIV). The curtain that separated man from

God was no longer and God became accessible to each and every believer. The priests were no longer necessary to communicate with the heavenly Father. Man was given the Holy Spirit as his guide and the Word of God as his map. Though spiritual leaders are still important today, they are not necessary to speak to God. When you are sanctified in the blood of Christ and consecrated with His Spirit and purpose, you have become a priest of the one true King. You have a direct line to the author of Creation, maker of Heaven and earth. Addiction is the repetition of sin, but you can be washed clean by the blood of the lamb. That does not mean that you are no longer a sinner or an addict; it means that you can live in the freedom of knowing that you have been acquitted. You have been made guiltless.

The blood from the purest lamb available was always used in sin offerings in Moses' day. It was even lamb's blood that was wiped on the entry ways during the Passover. This was such a powerful time in Judaism that the Passover is still celebrated to this day. The lamb's blood signified a mark of God's people and what was used to mark the homes of his people as the angel of death came past the Egyptians. So it was no wonder that in order to atone for man's sin, it took God himself stepping down on to the Earth being of no sin to become the lamb's blood needed to wash over us so the angel of evil would pass us by. This allowed us to be reconnected with our creator, God, and restore our relationship with Him. When God looks at us now, He sees His son and all that His son paid for with His blood.

We were built for relationships; why else would God want to walk with us in the garden, if not to have a relationship with us?

"Therefore, there is no condemnation for those who are in Christ Jesus," [Philippians 3:13]. It's an awesome reminder that I don't have to dwell on my mistakes but that I can truly let go of what is behind me and look forward.

"No test or temptation that comes your way is beyond the course of what others have had to face. All you need to remember is that God will never let you down; he'll never let you be pushed past your limit; he'll always be there to help you come through it."

1 Corinthians 10:13, The Message

Reflection Notes:

_____

_____

_____

_____

_____

_____

_____

_____

_____

_____

Journey Principle 5: "Impatience May Come, but Grace Will Follow."

Prayer

Aba (Father), thank you for this journey. Thank you for your principles, your wisdom, and your guidance. Thank you for showing me the road is long and the race is a marathon. Please calm my mind and heart and keep me steadfast in your purpose. Please help my impatient nature, but never let me lose my passion for you or your people. Help me know when I should just be still and know that you are God and when you want me to act. In Jesus' name, amen.

Stephen Scoggins

Journey Principle 5:
"Impatience May Come, but Grace Will Follow."

You roll over in bed and as you start to rest your head back on your pillow, you catch a brief glimpse of sunlight through the blinds...panic! You scramble for the clock on the nightstand knowing that the alarm was supposed to go off long before sunrise. Blinking numbers! There must have been a storm in the middle of the night that flickered the power. You jump out of bed, shower and get dressed in record time.

As you start the car, you remember that you forgot your coffee. No problem, you'll just hit the coffee shop on the way to work. Yes, you are already running late, but you are next to worthless without your cup of joe. You've been behind a school bus for four miles and now you are sitting at the seventh red light in between your house and caffeine. The light turns green... you can see the guy in front of you texting instead of looking at the light. Honk! Honk! Come on, buddy! Oh man, there are at least ten cars in the drive-thru. You run inside praying the line is shorter. Yup, only five people. Wait the second person in line is ordering for his entire office. The fourth person in line doesn't know what he wants even though he's been waiting fifteen minutes. The girl in front of you is digging around the bottom of her purse so she can find the exact change...you grab the coins from your pocket. "Here you go. No, please," hoping, praying...no, *insisting* that she take the seventeen cents from your outstretched palm.

Does this sound familiar? I'm sure that most of us have had a morning like that or some variation. Days like this happen to the best of us. Even though our circumstances may be our own creation or may not be anyone's fault at all, how quickly are we to become irritated and agitated with those who would appear to be slowing us down? I thought that my generation, Generation X, was bad, but Generation Y seems to have even less patience. Unfortunately, the problem is only perpetuated by a "me" society that is not just obsessed with instant gratification, but is developing the technology to supply it.

Are you hungry? Fast food. Need to go to the grocery

store, the line is too long? Self-checkout. Can't afford that new iPhone? Credit card. Don't have time to date? Look online or better yet, speed date. Oh man! What is that song that is playing right now? Shazam! I love it! Download. Listen to it three hundred times over the next three days and then never again. Can't remember the name of that actor from that movie? IMDb. But no, what was the line he said in that scene right before the...? Google. We have an app for that![5]

Impatience. It causes frustration, anger, resentment, and maybe even hostility. But what is it and where does it come from? I think that when most of us think about impatience, we think about a longing for the future. We feel excitement and anticipation for some upcoming experience that promises an emotional, physical, or material reward. However, we not only display impatience in reaching for the future, we also exhibit impatience to escape the present. Haven't you ever had a moment that you just wanted to get past? Maybe it was worry, embarrassment, or perhaps a moment of grief or pain, but you hoped and prayed that somehow, someway the clock would move just a little bit faster. Why do we want to escape the moment? Why do we want to rush to the future? Fear and greed. We either fear the moment or desire what we do not have. In both cases impatience can create unnecessary stress, can negatively affect your relationships, and can keep you from finding and experiencing joy in life.

~~~~~~~

I was on a trip to Nashville to visit my friends at Lampo. They have a fantastic business curriculum called EntreLeadership.

---

[5] For some reason when I think about the society that we live in, an image of Dustin Hoffman as Captain Hook pops into my head and I hear, "And you mindless, inexhaustible, unstoppable, repetitive, and nagging demands: He took my toy! She hit my bear! I want a potty! I want a cookie! I want to stay up! I want, I want, I want, me, me, me, me, mine, mine, mine, mine, now, now, now, now!" If you are in generation X, you get what I'm talking about. If you are in generation Y you probably saw the parentheses prior to this statement and skipped to the next paragraph because you are too impatient...And yes, I did Google that quote for the correct wording.

For those of you who are unfamiliar with that term, Lampo is the actual name of Dave and Sharon Ramsey's organization formed in 1992 after going into bankruptcy and losing everything. I will not try and tell Dave's story, but if at some point the opportunity presents itself, I highly recommend that you take full advantage of hearing how he and Sharon Ramsey have overcome their own obstacles on their journey.

Dave has developed a number of different practical application teaching tools, but one in particular, the EntreLeadership curriculum, has played an integral role in my life both personally and professionally.

Anyway, I have been blessed to share some time with key folks in their organization such as Chris Hogan, John Felkins, Daniel Tardy and many other awesome team members. Daniel Tardy is currently responsible for the "Entre" brand as of the time of writing this book.

On this particular trip, Daniel and his friend Seth invited me to work out with them. I am no stranger to the gym, but what Daniel hadn't told me was that he and Seth were training for a triathlon. Running, no problem. Swimming, I can handle that. Cycling...cycling is something that I had never really done before, and, to be honest, didn't necessarily care to try. However, when you have the chance to develop relationships with worthy mentors in your life, you want to get around them as much as possible to watch and grow. Tony Robbins calls this modeling in which you try to mimic and learn the character traits that have brought others success. I call it finding a mentor. This is a high-character person who will share the success and pitfalls of making radical life changes to improve your personal journey.

The cycling classes were intense and designed to test your endurance and your perseverance. However, the classes were full of bikers of all experience levels. There were no comparisons or judgments. No one expects anything from the other bikers in the room. You can coast through the entire class if you choose to or you can push yourself to your limits and see what you are made of. There is only you, your bike and your determination. There is no opponent...or is there? Everyone is just trying to beat his or her personal best and, to be honest, like most people you end up competing with the person next you. Daniel was next to me, and he is an experienced rider. I have to admit he owned me, but then I quickly realized who I was really competing against.

Watch out - here comes the sports metaphor (I think it's a requirement for every inspirational book!). But seriously, riding a bike is a lot like life. When you are riding, there are peaks and valleys, times to rest and times to grind. There are times to sit back and catch your breath and times to reach down deep to muster every single ounce of strength. The question is, what do you do when you meet the hills? Those obstacles are designed to test you. Your legs begin to burn and your face begins to sweat and before long, your body is numb and you are soaked. How do you react? Do you rise to the balls of your feet and push and grind? Or do you sit back, turn down the resistance on the bike and convince yourself that you aren't ready yet? It's too hard. I'm not strong enough. The other riders must be better prepared, stronger-willed...superior?

What is it that makes one person push and another coast? Pure heart, determination, and perseverance! The fact is that with each choice you condition your mind to make that choice easier the next time. Whether you shy away from the resistance or choose to meet it head-on, chances are that the same conclusion will come more quickly and easily the next time you meet an obstacle. The things that you tell yourself can do more good or bad than any words or tools fashioned against you. Your only limiting factor is you and the things that you choose to believe about yourself.

It is said "that perception is reality" and as you perceive the world, so shall it be. If your belief system is built around the potential that you see in yourself, it will drive the actions that you take. You must see the win in your mind's eye before you can ever obtain in the world's eyes. We were all made for a purpose and finding that purpose breeds fulfillment over time. You can buy the perfect bike shoes to help you stay in the stirrups or the water wicking clothes, but they are not going to make the difference between winning and losing. Focusing on your goal, pushing and grinding, and refusing to give up are the things that will keep you on your seat. *"Life is like a stationary bike."* When you get in the saddle, it may seem like you aren't actually going anywhere, but the work isn't about the destination; it's about strengthening your muscles, testing your limits, and perfecting your will and determination. Plain and simple. It's about growth and becoming a better you, physically, emotionally, and spiritually. I once heard someone say, "You will only be successful when you want to succeed as bad as you want to breathe." Yes, it is Eric Thomas again! Read that carefully my friends, "...as bad as you want to breathe." Have you ever had the wind knocked out of you? Have you felt the pain and the fear of trying to catch your breath? Life will bring those obstacles. There will be fear. There will be pain. There will be people who tell you that you aren't good enough, strong enough, or not smart enough. It is in those moments that you must rise to the balls of your feet, bare down and focus. Drive one leg forward and then the other, again and again and again.

~~~~~~~

How many times have you heard "life is a series of moments?" or "you can own the moment or let the moment own you"? The fact is that some of the simplest truths get overlooked because we see them or hear them every day in movies, on T-shirts, and bumper stickers. Once you begin to hear things over and over, they slowly start to lose something...but life *is* a series of moments! Some may hold a little more excitement than others, but each is profound in and of itself. Each moment holds within it a chance to grow to become better, stronger, and smarter. Impatience robs you of the moment. Because of your fear or greed, you allow yourself to be cheated of an opportunity for self-discovery, of self-actualization.

We live in an age where time is money, do we not? I spoke earlier about how we grow impatient because we perceive a future moment to hold some emotional or material reward. It is in the comparison of value between the present and the future that causes us to be impatient. I have realized that the only person I want to be better tomorrow than I was today is "me".[6] Follow me for a second. We long for the future because we believe that there is something there waiting for us that is better than the place we currently stand. We become so focused on that prospective gain that all the moments between now and then become annoying, frustrating or even angering. But what is it that we are really searching for? Why is it that we even assign value in the first place? I had to think long and hard about that question. There was a long progression before I reached my conclusion, but long story short, we assign value based on demand and desire for a product or service. However, the desire is the direct result of a perceived happiness that the product or service will supply. At the end of the day, everybody has something to sell and is always selling happiness. The problem is it's a false perception of happiness. I believe true happiness is only found inside Gods will and in His purpose.

Worldview - Happiness is an important part of life, so much so that even the U.S. Declaration of Independence describes it as that which should be pursued. However, I would argue that happiness is merely a byproduct of contentment. Contentment is our building block for this principle. Contentment recognizes that just as much can be gained from pain and suffering as success and accomplishment. While happiness can be fleeting, contentment is consistent. Happiness asks for more, but contentment is always satisfied. Contentment is the great equalizer because when you can find satisfaction and happiness in any circumstance, you essentially remove the perceived value of worldly happiness and completely bypass any potential for exhibiting impatience.

Faith Perspective – We live in a world that is insatiable which is perhaps nowhere more evident than here in the States where consumerism and materialism are the economical foundation of

---

[6] Just an FYI, this is not going to be a rant on capitalism. Just as people with differing views than our own help us to refine our own belief structure, I also believe that economical competition breeds success. Perhaps a topic for another book.

our society. I'm not saying having things or desiring things makes you a bad person, but I will ask you where your heart is. Are your desires genuine or are they jealous? Are the things that you own a status symbol, purchased with pride? I'm not here to judge anyone based on what they have. Who am I to question the ways in which the Lord has blessed you? Can I ask if your faith is as strong when you are being challenged as when you are being blessed? Paul tells us in Philippians 4:12-13 "I know what it is to be in need, and I know what it is to have plenty. I have learned the secret of being content in any and every situation, whether well fed or hungry, whether living in plenty or in want. I can do all this through Him who gives me strength." [NIV]

So my caution is not in what you own or the state of your portfolio, but in where you find your strength. If the things that you own end up owning you and your identity is defined by what you have instead of who you are, then you have lost sight of your calling. Jesus tells us "Therefore I tell you, do not worry about your life, what you will eat or drink; or about your body, what you will wear. Is not life more important than food, and the body more important than clothes?" [Matthew 6:25, NIV]. The Lord knows our needs and He is our supply. He is faithful in His provision. Find contentment in the Father and rest in His mercies.

...For the pagans run after all these things, and your heavenly Father knows that you need them. But seek first his kingdom and his righteousness, and all these things will be given to you as well"

Matthew 6:25, 32-22

Reflective Notes:

_____

_____

_____

_____

_____

_____

_____

_____

_____

I ONCE WAS LOST,
BUT NOW I'M FOUND

"My son," the father said, "you are always with me, and everything
I have is yours."

Luke 15.31

Journey Principle 6: "Sorrow is an Illusion"

Prayer

Father, how great is your plan. How great is your mission for my life. I know that you bring forth all things for your plan and you waste nothing. Please walk with me now releasing in my heart and mind all sorrow and pain. Please reveal to me how you want it to be a part of my walk, plan and testimony. Remove doubt from me and cast it away in the deepest sea, never to be seen again. I can now see sorrow has no purpose in my life any longer, and I can see how the evil has made it a plan to keep me from that which you created me for. Help me to realize not my worth in others, but my worth in you! In Jesus' name, amen.

Stephen Scoggins

Journey Principle 6:
"Sorrow is an Illusion"

In *The Prophet*, Khalil Gibran states, "Some of you say, 'Joy is greater than sorrow,' and others say, 'Nay, sorrow is the greater.' But I say unto you, they are inseparable. Together they come and when one sits alone with you at your board, remember that the other is asleep upon your bed." Sorrow comes to us all. It is an inescapable part of life and unfortunately, the longer you live the more likely you are to experience it. I think that Gibran hits the nail on the head in his association between sorrow and joy because we do not miss or grieve for that which we have not enjoyed. We notice when joy is taken from us. We miss it. We yearn for it. Its absence creates pain. Just as each moment of joy is unique in and of itself, so is every circumstance surrounding pain and the ways in which each of us experience and cope with that sorrow. Despite our differences, the one thing that seems to hold true for each of us is that time heals all wounds.

I think that many of us associate grief and sorrow with the loss of a loved one. Sorrow is not limited to death alone, but to loss in a whole. When a marriage or a friendship ends, we grieve. We feel pain when we lose a job or maybe when the doctor gives us bad news concerning ourselves or a loved one. We have all heard stories of someone who couldn't fulfill their life dream because of an unexpected medical condition. Or the superstar athlete whose performance becomes almost embarrassing because they didn't have the strength to walk away from the game. When we are forced to face the fact that something is coming to an end, sorrow steps in, takes over and makes it so that even the most simple tasks and decisions become challenging.

Most of you are probably familiar with the five stages of grief developed by psychiatrist Elisabeth Kübler-Ross, in which she describes the transition through the grieving process. But just in case you are not familiar with them, here is a quick summary:

1. **Denial:** The disbelief that this is happening.
2. **Anger:** Trying to figure out why it is happening.
3. **Bargaining:** If someone can just make this go away, I will do or give...
4. **Depression:** The pain is too much to bear.
5. **Acceptance:** You have finally found peace.

I want to point out that the stages are not definitive. Everyone's path to healing is different. Not everyone experiences each of the stages and neither do they necessarily happen in order and some may go through certain stages multiple times before ever reaching acceptance. The observation that I want to make involves the relationship between the four stages before acceptance. What do they all have in common? Come on, you know this! Yup, it's fear! In case you haven't noticed, fear is a recurring theme in this book. I hope you are starting to understand that, ultimately, every negative emotion that you have the capability of feeling breaks down to fear or, at least, has a fear component. Sorrow is no different. We fear change. We fear finality. Loss can make us feel anxious or insecure or can even make us question our own mortality. However, one of the things that I believe people fear most is their ability to find joy beyond the sorrow. This is especially true in the loss of a loved one. Not only do we miss them, but also we fear our ability to replace the joy and eventually the guilt of trying to do so.

After my mother's attempted suicide, she spent some time in an institution and then moved to Kentucky and into yet another bad relationship. My Nanny became the official guardian for my brother and me; at least, it felt that way. Then when I was around the age of nine, my Nanny was diagnosed with cancer. It started in her lungs. The culprit was probably those skinny little cigarettes that she loved so much.

Over the next two years she battled, stuck in a revolving door of sickness and remission. I remember her coming home from chemo, just a shell of her former self, frail and fatigued. Even though she could barely move around the house, she made sure to teach me to make oatmeal, hot dogs, mac and cheese, and a few other dishes that were simple. I guess she knew what was coming and that it was important that I learned to take care of myself and my brother. Soon I was getting my brother up and ready for school, making breakfast, lunches, or anything else that would help to take the strain off of Nanny.

Eventually, the chemo took its toll. Nanny's hair was now gone, and she was constantly getting sick to her stomach. I was doing the best I could to help, but it became necessary for Nanny's sister, Aunt Mickey, to move in with us. A four-foot-nothing spitfire, She was a tiny little thing who, in spite of her emphysema, still smoked a pack a day. Man, was she stubborn, but she also brought a whole lot of fun into a house that hadn't seen any in some time. God has a funny way of mixing in joy with the sorrow.

Finally, things got so bad that my mother and father had to come back to North Carolina. My father stayed with family in a nearby town, but my mother stayed with us. She stayed by her mother's bedside and helped however she could. It was the first time I saw my mother and Nanny be like a real mother and daughter. They were completely different with each other over the next few months...the last few months. This was my first experience of seeing what a mother-daughter relationship should be like, and later would be yet one more reason why healthy relationships became a focus of mine. God has a funny way of bringing healing with the pain.

Things finally got so bad that Nanny needed full-time care. It was so strange to see someone I love, who was once very strong and able-bodied lying in a hospital bed. Tubes were coming out of her nose and connected to ventilator-style machines. For a little while, the images of her from the hospital gave me nightmares. I would wake up in the middle of the night afraid that it was me with the needles in my arm with tubes coming from everywhere and connected to the machines, but I didn't let that stop me from going to visit my Nanny. Even at that age, I could sense how important those last moments were. I could see her through the doorway in her hospital room before she knew I was there. I could hardly recognize her, but something changed when she saw me and my brother. She sat up! I don't know where the energy came from or how she managed to do it, but she sat up and lit up with that never-failing smile that couldn't be masked by tubes or by pain, that smile that spoke straight to my heart and told me that everything was going to be okay, that soon, very soon, everything was going to be better. God has a funny way of instilling clarity in times of great confusion.

One day, out of nowhere, my uncle showed up to take Ryan and I on a camping trip. He used to take us when we were younger, but I hadn't seen him in a while, and the timing felt off. Of course, in retrospect, the timing makes perfect sense. Ryan and I had a great couple of days with our uncle, but the car ride home was unusually quiet. We pulled back into our driveway in silence and walked into the house to find my mother sitting at the kitchen in the black chair...Nanny's chair. She was visibly shaken, but did her best to hold it together as she waved at us to come to her. We climbed up into the chairs on either side of her. She took us each by the hand and began to tell us how Nanny was no longer with us and that she had gone to Heaven. My heart ached and all that I could think about was how I wished I could have just one more hug! Then I remembered her smile in the hospital and a wave of peace rushed over me and I knew that she was safe and no longer in pain.

Sorrow and grief come to us all. For some of us, it comes earlier in life than we could have ever expected. I was only nine. While I was given some peace about Nanny's passing, I still missed her more than I had ever missed anything. Without a doubt, up until the moment that she was gone and perhaps even until now, she may have been the most important person in my life, my first example of love and dedication. At that time, there was no way for me to see all of the ways that her life had influenced mine. I do see the effects of her love and influence in the many ways I might react to some situations. In my words and when I make eye contact with someone, I recognize that my smile might be that person's strength for the day. It's true that you never know what you have until it is gone, but isn't that the irony about sorrow, that it makes you realize how important something or someone is to you? It forces you to calculate the significance. Even though you are in pain and grieving, you know that the extent of your sorrow is a direct correlation of the love and joy that had been placed in your life. Life *is* a series of moments and, ultimately, about how we respond to those moments. Denial, anger, bargaining, and depression might seem like appropriate responses to sorrow. Nobody wants to experience loss and pain. Nobody wishes to have joy and love stolen from their lives. No matter what your beliefs may be about what waits for us all beyond death, the simple truth is that this life is one of impermanence. Stating that fact to someone who is grieving is obviously a poor approach to comfort, but training yourself to experience life with this understanding will not only help you to better appreciate your blessings, but it may make the grieving process a little easier when the time comes.

Sorrow, like any other obstacle in life, is a chance for you to define yourself. If you let it, if you confront it, it will allow you to better understand who you are and, more importantly, who you want to be. It can simultaneously make you aware of your strengths and what areas of your life have room for improvement. It can help refine your perspective and reshape your priorities. Since time heals all wounds, sorrow forces you to practice patience and perseverance. Sorrow humbles you. Last, but not least, sorrow reminds you that life is fragile and fleeting, but it will help you to recognize and appreciate the joy in your life.

In a principle that has worked so hard to create a relationship between joy and sorrow, you might think that joy would be the obvious building block. You would be right, but it's not the topic that I want to pursue. I really thought very hard about the building block for this principle. As you can see from the previous paragraph, there are so many profound and insightful lessons to be taken from sorrow that it was actually difficult for me to narrow it down to a single choice. The more I thought about the takeaways; I realized that there was something very important that I overlooked. Yes, sorrow can teach *you* patience. It can teach *you* humility. It can give *you* perspective. Your personal experience with pain and grief can teach *you* so many things, but while your experience is unique, sorrow is something that every single one of us share. So what do we take from sorrow that goes beyond ourselves? What can we learn from our pain that transcends our own personal experience to impact humanity's collective sorrow positively? Compassion!

Compassion (Worldview) - While our individual sorrow may be subjective, the emotion itself is something that each and every one of us share. The understanding of the pain and the struggle that accompany sorrow is something that should pull us together. Compassion doesn't look at our petty differences. It doesn't look at skin color. It doesn't look at gender. It doesn't see philosophy, theology, or politics. Compassion takes a direct route to the things that we have in common, the things that connect us, and completely bypass anything and everything that might separate us. Compassion not only unifies, but, if you let it, fortifies!

> *"Our human compassion binds us the one to the other – not in pity or patronizingly, but as human beings who have learnt how to turn our common suffering into hope for the future."* Nelson Mandela

Developing your sympathy, empathy, and compassion for others will completely change your perspective on life and how you interact with those around you. Start to look for ways that you can practice compassion as Mandela said. Not from pity, but from a genuine desire to better understand what others may be going through.

Compassion (Faith Perspective) - Compassion is a useful tool in helping to shoulder the load of our brothers and sisters in Christ. Compassion might just be the greatest tool in redeeming the lost. You can preach 'til the cows come home, but nothing displays the love of the Father and speaks to the hearts of man like genuine compassion. As Christians, we are commissioned for compassion!

What do you think inspired Jesus to come down and walk this earth as a man? Why do you think He traveled from town to city, city to town, sharing the truth of His Father? Why do you think He healed the sick, raised the dead, cleansed the lepers, and drove out demons[7]? What made Him feed the five thousand, speak to the woman at the well, and draw a line in the sand? What was He teaching the disciples when He washed their feet? What made Jesus tell Peter to sheathe his sword so that He could heal the ear of the guard knowing all too well where the Romans would be taking Him? Why did He accept the nails and the crown of thorns upon His head? Because the greatest love story of all time is a story of compassion!

---

[7] Matthew 10:8

Gracious is the LORD, and righteous; Yes, our God is compassionate.

Psalms 116:5, NASB

Reflective Notes:

_____

_____

_____

_____

_____

_____

_____

_____

_____

_____

Journey Principle 7: "Pride's Prison"

Prayer

Father, you have always said pride comes before the fall. Remove pride from my life. Grant in me a clean heart and right spirit, never denying my heart from any of your love, grace and mercy you have to offer. Help me to serve, and not be selfish. Help me to grow in washing the feet of others as You wash my heart of pride. Clean me, oh Lord. Restore me, oh Lord. Let pride not tear me from you, from others or my utter and complete healing. In Jesus' name, Amen.

Stephen Scoggins

Journey Principle 7:
"Pride's Prison"

Pride is different from the other obstacles we have encountered so far because it isn't always a bad thing. In fact, pride in the sense of having dignity or honor is a very good thing. There is an extremely fine line between dignity and arrogance and, unfortunately, it seems like the latter is often easier for us find. What is it about human nature that allows us to let things go to our heads so quickly?

I believe the answer to that is simple and it is a topic we have already explored: greed. I truly believe that every wrong action derives from greed and choosing self. This is especially true with pride. Pride is different, because it can be both positive and negative; we must seek and distinguish the point that it changes. We must learn to recognize how and why our dignity becomes arrogance, our integrity becomes vanity and our honor conceit.

It feels good to receive praise and to have someone tell you that you did a good job. There is absolutely nothing wrong with being proud of your accomplishments. Having pride in who you are, what you have overcome and in the ways you have triumphed is an important part of becoming who you were meant to be.

Pride can be an integral step in self-actualization. Not just merely allowing you to see your value as an individual, but also your potential. Pride can be a driving force that pushes you toward future success. It inspires creativity. It forces you to dream. Pride fuels the fire of ambition. As life moves forward and more problems arise, you will return to your pride, to your past victories, to draw strength for your current battle. You will remember, and the seed of hope will bud into courage and then flower into perseverance. Pride can help you to maintain your standards, forcing you to stick to your moral and ethical guns. Pride can simultaneously come from and create joy, perpetuating the pursuit of happiness.

So how can the potential for so much good become something so bad? That very thin line is crossed when we are no longer content in our achievements, when praise moves from simply being accepted to being sought out, and when we begin to look outside of our own journey and begin to contrast ourselves with those around us. It is inevitable. It is who we are. It is in our nature to ultimately look outside of our circumstances and experience life in comparison to others. It is within that comparison that we find the change from being proud (positive) to becoming prideful (negative).

When something negative happens in your life, by accident or a mistake, what is your reaction? Do you consider the possibility that it may be you who is in error or do you blame others for your misfortunes? Do you brag about your possessions or your accomplishments? Have you ever stretched the truth in order to gain more recognition for your achievements or have you lied or deceived in order to minimize someone else's success and promote yourself? Are you quick to judge others because of the way they dress, think, or act differently than you do? Are you open to accepting wisdom from others or do you know it all?

"Pride gets no pleasure out of having something, only out of having more of it than the next man." C.S. Lewis

We live in a society that is in a race. A race to have more, do more or be better than those around us. It's so unfortunate, but many people can only perceive their value in comparison to others. They are so lost. They don't know who they are or what they stand for. They are so discontent with what they have that the only way they can experience joy or happiness is by creating a mindset that lifts their circumstances above others. This mindset is not joy! No matter how much you try and fool yourself, this is not happiness. It is pride and an extremely unhealthy way to assign value to one's life.

Normally we wait just a little bit further into the principle to assign a building principle. However, because pride can be both good and bad I believe that one of the best ways to try and define it is to show what it is not. Our principle for this principle is humility. I normally try to take a different angle than the obvious antonym, but humility is such an essential concept for all walks of life and at the same time tough to understand, difficult to practice, and challenging to maintain. We are prideful beings and humility is not only hard for us, but there is also the pitfall of trying too hard. And guess what? Displaying a false-humility is just another form of pride.

"There is nothing noble in being superior to your fellow man; true nobility is being superior to your former self."
Ernest Hemingway

This is a profound observation from Mr. Hemingway and if we focus on a few of the key words in this statement, we can gain great insight into becoming a more humble person. When you look at the second half of this quote what are the words that stand out to you or the words that you feel carry the most weight? In my opinion, the words "true," "superior," and "former" are what give this phrase steam, and I want to explore them in reverse.

First, the word "former" has a number of implications, but the most obvious is that change or transformation must occur. There is a "becoming" suggested here, a transformation that implies leaving behind a state that is less desirable than the object of your pursuit. It is extremely important that a person recognize the need for change. Without diagnosing the reasons for change, where you stand and where you wish to be, the less likely that the change will stick and the more likely you are to return to your old ways. Change is not always easy, but it's like pulling off a band-aid--it's better to commit to it and make a move or else you will experience more pain in the long run.

"Stepping onto a brand-new path is difficult, but not more difficult than remaining in a situation, which is not nurturing to the whole [person]." Maya Angelou

Second, and building off of the first, the word "superior" tells us that the person that we will become is better than what we were. That's sort of obvious, but I want to take it a step further.

81

Finding your superior self, becoming a better you, implies becoming stronger. When you change, you grow and when you grow, you get stronger. It's a little ironic, especially in a world where many believe that humility is a sign of weakness. However, becoming a more humble person gives you strength. Sometimes it is difficult to perceive, but there are numerous ways in which humility empowers you. Think, if you will, about living a life where you do not feel the need to impress those around you, a life where you are content in yourself. What things in your life would change? Would you have less stuff, fewer material possessions? Would you drive a different car or live in a different house? How do you think that living a more modest lifestyle would impact you financially and how would that influence your life? Maybe you would have less stress, be able to travel more or be able to give and serve more. Now, think about having the ability to approach every situation, person, and conversation without having the need to be right. I'm certainly not implying that you need to allow yourself and your views to be trampled, but how would simply changing your approach to one of humility and respect change the relationships in your life? Would you judge people less and appreciate people more? How might it affect your ability to forgive? Would you be a better listener? Doesn't it feel like we live in a society where people are just waiting for their turn to talk?

Becoming a better listener doesn't just strengthen you, but it empowers those around you. Think about how our society would change with fewer people who felt misunderstood, free from judgment and more confident in expressing emotion. What tragedies might we avoid? Finally, how do you think humility might affect your ability to confront obstacles? After all, this is exactly what this book is about: how to engage conflict. How would life's discouragements, losses, and pain impact a humble person? I want you to think about that for a moment. Humility is a game changer because it completely transforms your perception of reality. Again, while some look at it as a weakness, in truth, there is great strength in humility because it can give you absolute and complete freedom over your circumstances.

Last, I want to look at the word "true." If I asked you the meaning of the word, what might you say? Accurate, legitimate, honest, loyal? All of those are correct. There's not a wrong answer here. "True" is just one of those words that has so many meanings that it probably takes up a full page in a thesaurus. However, in Mr. Hemingway's quote, "true" modifies "nobility" which is in reference to "self," so I think it is a safe observation to say that what we are talking about here is character. When I think about having "true character," I take all those words from the thesaurus, study them, and break them down and I feel like they are all chiefly represented by two main principles: consistency and sincerity.

A person can be sincere, but inconsistent, and a person can be consistently insincere. Together, consistency and sincerity make for greatness of character! But what does that say about humility, you might ask? The first point we have already explored briefly and it is that insincere humility is not humility at all. It is only another form of pride. False humility is hypocrisy which is a prideful person pretending to be humble in order to receive some emotional gain.

I was on Facebook the other day and I saw someone who had "checked in" at a soup kitchen and posted nothing other than the single word "volunteering." For those of you who may be unfamiliar with Facebook or the term "checking in," it is basically a feature that utilizes the GPS on your phone to make a post on Facebook that puts a big "X" on a map and says, "I am here!". In my opinion, it's the most prideful and narcissistic Facebook post next to the "selfie," of course. Yes, I have taken selfies before and also checked in at places to let others know I was there.

Please remember this book is about all life has taught me and others through my personal journey, and I am by no means saying I am not guilty of the exact things I am now discussing.

I quickly realized that making that sort of post on Facebook goes completely against the intended action of serving others. Turning it into something about yourself in some ways undermines the good deed itself. When people do things like go into in a crowded room and say things for others to hear or acting out on Facebook, these are in fact a sign of low self-esteem. We are all trying to find our value by making ourselves feel important.

The Bible in Proverbs says clearly that we should avoid praising ourselves and let our actions be pure and of good heart. Humility seeks to aid, promote, and lift up others out of genuine and sincere concern for their wellbeing. It is not self-seeking, self-promoting, or self-aggrandizing. The second point, consistency, is the closest that we can come to an ideal. An ideal such as humility is an absolute and it is perfect. As imperfect beings who exist in change, the closest that we can get to perfection is to act with consistency. Tony Robbins notes, "It's not what we do once in a while that shapes our lives. It's what we do consistently." I couldn't agree more!

I have said it before and I will say it again: our decisions define us and the ways in which we display consistency are what create our character. Tony Robbins had another great shift when he said "It is not what we do or have that define us, it's who we become". It has to stop being about the praise, the stuff, the economic justification, and more about the journey and becoming something more than we were yesterday.

Now that we have looked at how those three words can give us some great insight as to how view and practice humility, I want to look at what I believe to be a great take away from Hemingway's quote. The overarching concept is that the difference between humility and pride lies in the competition of our hearts. Who are we competing with? If you look at Hemingway's statement, he doesn't say that competition is a bad thing, he asks with whom we are in competition. Are you living your life in comparison of others or are you in competition with yourself to become a more "superior" you? When you can take your eyes off of everyone else's journey and focus on your own, then you have truly given yourself the freedom to grow and reach your full potential.

Humility (Worldview) – Take a moment and think about all the negative emotions that come from a having a prideful heart. Arrogance, egotism, vanity, and discontent are the obvious ones, but did you think about resentment, annoyance, complacency, boastfulness, suspicion, jealousy, and bitterness? I could keep going. Sophocles said, "All men make mistakes, but a good man yields when he knows his course is wrong and repairs the evil. The only crime is pride." Sophocles states that pride is the cause of all wrongdoing. I personally believe that greed is the chief cause of sin, but I suppose that you could make the argument that pride and greed are essentially one and the same: choosing self.

Here are some action steps to help overcome self and choose humility:

1. **Humility values others** and their perspectives. We must understand that each person brings their own special gifts to the table. Every person has something valuable to contribute and so every person deserves respect. We have talked about iron sharpening iron and the war of conflicting ideas. Teaching the best way for us to grow as individuals and as a collective is to learn from each other's strengths and to build off of them.
2. **Recognize your weaknesses.** John C. Maxwell states that, "Pride deafens us to the advice or warnings of those around us." When you humbly accept your limitations, it opens up your heart and mind to receive wisdom from those around you.
3. **Humility isn't about promoting yourself**; it's about improving you! Remember to focus your eyes on you and your journey and not to live a life in comparison of others.

Humility (Faith Perspective) – There are so many places I could point to for a Christian perspective on humility. The quote I gave you from C.S. Lewis earlier in the principle is from a section in *Mere Christianity* where Lewis contrasts pride and

85

humility. I highly recommend Saint Augustine's *Confessions* in which Augustine, like Sophocles, describes pride as the genesis of all sin. Saint Benedict has a twelve-step program up the mountain of pride and another to humility. However, as Christians, our focus should always remain on Christ who is always our best example and so I turn to Philippians:

> Therefore if you have any encouragement from being united with Christ, if any comfort from his love, if any common sharing in the Spirit, if any tenderness and compassion, then make my joy complete by being like-minded, having the same love, being one in spirit and of one mind. Do nothing out of selfish ambition or vain conceit. Rather, in humility value others above yourselves, not looking to your own interests but each of you to the interests of the others. In your relationships with one another, have the same mindset as Christ Jesus: Who, being in very nature God, did not consider equality with God something to be used to his own advantage; rather, he made himself nothing by taking the very nature of a servant, being made in human likeness. And being found in appearance as a man, he humbled himself by becoming obedient to death—even death on a cross! (Philippians 2:1-8, NIV)

For everyone who exalts themselves will be humbled, and they who humble themselves will be exalted."

Luke 14:11

Reflective Notes:

_____

_____

_____

_____

_____

_____

_____

_____

_____

Journey Principle 8: "Guilt Has Had Us Long Enough"

Prayer

Father, please grant me revelation - revelation of my mind and spirit. I know that you sent your personal best in Jesus so I would no longer have to be burdened with the mistakes I have made on my journey, no longer burdened with the pain of the damage I have inflicted others. Please touch their hearts and let them hear my cry of apology. Most of all, Father, remind me each day that Jesus paid it all. And all to him I owe! In Jesus' name, amen.

Stephen Scoggins

Journey Principle 8:
"Guilt Has Had Us Long Enough"

Guilt. It is an extremely powerful emotion. Webster's Dictionary defines guilt as "(1) the fact of having committed a breach of conduct, especially violating law and involving a penalty, and (2) the state of one who has committed an offense, especially consciously." There are two aspects as to how guilt affects us. Firstly, the state of being guilty comes from doing something wrong. Secondly, there are the emotions that follow as a result of knowing that we have done wrong. So guilt is both something we do and how we feel. The question is to what extent should we feel guilt, if at all? Well let me tell you, if you are feeling guilt it just means that you are normal. In fact, a person who lacks feelings of guilt or remorse is the definition of a sociopath. Guilt is necessary. It's our body's way, both physically and mentally, of making us aware that we have done wrong. However, at what point does guilt stop being useful and start becoming harmful? I believe to get to the bottom of that question we must fully define what guilt is by distinguishing it from its extensions: regret, shame, and conviction.

Regret and guilt, at first glance, appear to be similar. However, they are quite different. Guilt is the result of knowing that what you are doing is wrong and doing it anyway. Regret, on the other hand, doesn't have that original awareness. It's more of an afterthought or hindsight, wishing that you had done something differently. The way I like to look at it is that regret is usually the product of ignorance or indifference, while guilt is almost always flat out rebellion.

Shame is at the other end of the spectrum from regret. It isn't an afterthought; it is constant. It is a dangerous perception that not only have you done wrong, but that you will continue to do wrong because there is something wrong with you. I hope that I don't need to point out how self-destructive this is. Nonetheless, this difference points out a very specific distinction, that guilt recognizes within itself the ability to change whereas shame is completely negative. It feels trapped without a way out.

Conviction is extremely similar to guilt. To be honest, the majority of people might argue that they aren't just similar, but they are one and the same. I would agree, except for one distinction and that is that I believe that guilt is internal and conviction is external. Conviction comes from an outside source: a friend, family member, society, or a judge and jury telling you that what you did was wrong. You become convinced that you were in error. Guilt, as I said with regret, almost always comes from knowing what the right thing to do is, but making the wrong choice anyway. This very small difference between being internal and external, however, has very large implications for how we view and experience guilt because it brings the topic of blame to the forefront. We live in a society that loves to point fingers. We are so quick to shift the blame from ourselves and not accept responsibility for our actions. Very often, we catch ourselves telling others not to make us feel guilty.

Well, in my experience, we might try and shift the blame to others by telling them not to make us feel guilty, but if you're already feeling guilt, it's coming from your own heart.

Side note: I want to be clear here that I am talking about genuine personal guilt. I know that there are relationships where individuals are mentally/emotionally abused into feeling guilty about things for which they are not at fault. I am not talking about those instances in which someone might be forced into a false perception of guilt.

Now that we have shaped a better definition of guilt, let's look at how these distinctions can help us see the difference between guilt's utility and when it becomes destructive. We have learned from regret that we feel guilt from consciously choosing what we know to be wrong. When we accept this feeling in a healthy and constructive way, the first thing we are doing is taking responsibility for our actions. That accountability will result in seeking forgiveness and making amends. From shame, we have learned that guilt can see this process as an opportunity for healing and growth. However, you must still make the choice for growth. Dave Grohl says, "Guilt is cancer. Guilt will confine you, torture you, destroy you...It's a black wall. It's an [expletive] thief." Ignoring guilt is toxic. It will eat away at you and, as Dave said, it can steal from you, eating away at your integrity, peace, and joy just to name a few. Finally, we looked at conviction as being external and at guilt as being internal. This reinforces taking responsibility for our actions by remembering that sincere guilt comes from within, but when taking the healthy approach, it should also open up our perspectives beyond our own personal feelings by taking into consideration the feelings of others. Just because we may not feel guilt, it doesn't mean that we are not guilty. Be welcoming when others attempt to share how your words and/or actions have affected them. Perhaps you didn't realize that you were in the wrong, or you honestly feel as if you are in the right. Show compassion for their pain and seek restitution. This is another opportunity for healing and growth.

~~~~~~~

In the fall of 1996, I was working for a man named Steve Myrick. Steve served in WWII as a Merchant Marine and when the war was over, he moved to Raleigh, North Carolina where he became a sub-contractor. In a little over fifty years, Steve developed forty-two subdivisions in the greater Raleigh area. He was only 5'5," but he was an extremely tough and smart businessman. As tough as he could be, he was an extremely humble man. He had a number of crews that worked for him. On most paydays he would drive out and personally hand each man his check, shake their hand, and thank them for the work they had done.

The time that I worked for Steve was one of the times that I severely dealt with depression. I was on a job for Steve by myself, when I just began crying. I'm not sure what it was exactly that made me cry, but when you are dealing with depression, there doesn't even have to be a specific reason. It just happens sometimes. This was during the time of the girl from the Barbecue place and this instance happened to be particularly bad. So bad, in fact, that I just began walking. I had a company truck that was right there, but I began walking and continued to walk until I made it all the way to the single-wide trailer that I was living in at the time. I did not leave that trailer for the next week. I didn't sleep, but I never got out of bed.

That was a rough week for me. The depression was already difficult, but the guilt of walking off the job that was given to me by a man whom I both admired and respected tore me apart. Steve had taught me a lot, but one of the things that had stuck with me was that "If you make one person happy he will tell ten, but if you make one person angry he will tell one hundred."

My guilt was forcing me to think about how angry I had made Steve and whom he might be telling.

A little over a year passed and I had still not talked to Steve, but the circumstances of my life had put me in a position where I had nothing and needed to find work (the story coming in Principle 10). My father, who was employed with Steve, went to him on my behalf and let him know that I was looking for a job. My father was able to get Steve to allow me back on a framing crew. The next day, my father took me to Lowes and bought me the only tools he could afford to help me with: a hammer, a white nail apron (*not a set of nice nail pouches),* and framing square. This, all-in-all, may have been about thirty dollars, but it was enough to get me going and at least back to a nine dollar-an-hour position. This was a far cry from what I had been making with the siding business Steve tried to help me start originally.

Just about a week later it was pay day and I had not seen Steve at all. In fact, as he would circle the neighborhood, as he often did, I would hide as I would see him coming. I was still full of all kinds of guilt and shame. To make matters even worse, I was able to watch the guys who took my place work each day with my old tools which he sold to them after I left and went on my long walk.

Later that day, I was working reframing a garage door and overheard the siding guys say something about not showing up Monday because Steve had not paid them all of their money on the check they just received. They were wanting final payment on a home that was not even done! I was enraged! How could they hurt the man who had done everything right? How could someone do such a thing? Then a quiet whisper said, *"Didn't you do the same thing?"* I quickly realized this was a voice of guilt and shame. I did not know at the time, but God allowed me to stare my mistake square in the eyes and even allow me to make a different choice. I am not sure if it was anger or the Holy Spirit, but I was finally ready to face my fear, anxiety, guilt and depression. I was ready face my mentor and a father figure to me: Steve Myrick.

I remember it like it was yesterday. I simply walked up to Steve, and he asked, "How's your head feeling now' a days, boy?" He didn't just come out and say everything that he wanted, I am sure, but what he really wanted to know was where my life was. I thought for sure I was walking into a cursing or at minimum a lecture, but I got none of that. I got only a humble smile and a question. "I'm working on it, sir." I couldn't just come out and tell him that I wasn't too far off from where I was two years ago. In regards to my financial condition, it was just now getting possible to eat. It helped that the week before my father had allowed me to crash on his couch. However, my heart was different.

Steve and I had an interesting relationship. It had always been like a grandfather-grandson relationship. In our one sentence exchange, we told each other a great deal. The truth is that he could probably see it. Steve was an excellent judge of character. I began to tell Steve what I had previously overheard from the siding installers. I felt my spirit say, 'Ask him!' I paused and stared for what seem like an eternity.

The air conditioner was blowing out Steve's white Jeep Grand Cherokee window; it was blowing on my face and in what felt like a 90-degree day, it felt awesome. Again, I heard 'Ask Him!' so I did my best to muster up the courage and said, "Steve, if they don't come back on Monday, can I take over?" I am not sure who was more stunned, Steve or me, at what came out of my mouth. Steve paused for a moment and then chuckled and said, "How are you going to do that? I sold the tools to the guys over there, and they are not mine. Also you don't have any helpers or trucks and you only have that little white tool belt."

He was right! I did not have any of those things. I held the first paycheck I'd had in a long while, and it wasn't much over two hundred dollars.

I am truly not sure what it was inside of me, but I felt like I owed it to him, and most of all I owed it to myself. I could feel God urging me to trust Him on this and God did say if you are faithful with little I will make you faithful over much. So, this is one time in my life when faith is all I went on! I simply told Steve to please let me do it and I would figure it out.

Steve laughed and said, "Ok, if they don't come back on Monday, you can finish that house and we can go from there." I was both excited and terrified; I just made a seemingly impossible deal to a man I had already wronged once. I did not have any tools or people. I began to ask myself, 'What was I thinking?' Then a calm came over me and I heard a voice almost audibly say, 'Son, be still and know that He is God.' Was it my grandfather who led me back to the cross many years ago and who I still hear speak wisdom to me? Or was it God? Funny...my grandfather's voice in my brain sounds a lot like I would think God sounds like.

I know the events after that made it undeniable that God was present. I told my father what had happened and he was visibly upset. I think he thought I would fail again. After knowing about the ordeal I had just gone through, he was scared to death for me. He said, "You need to go tell him it's not a great idea and get out of it." I still felt in my heart of hearts it was the right thing to do. It also made me ask a question, and that is how many people try and talk us out of succeeding because they are afraid of our failure or more importantly our success? My father being the man he was said, "OK, let's try and figure it out." This was the first time I had ever felt supported or important to my father. You know what he did? He didn't give me money; he didn't give tools! He said, "Do you remember working with granddad Scoggins during the summers?" I told him I did and He asked if I remembered the wood scaffolding we used. "Yes," I exclaimed. "Ok, then start pulling wood out of the trash piles. We have scaffolds to build!"

We spent the entire weekend building the tools I would

need to get started and then he took me to buy three red old school scaffold bucks and rent a break machine for bending metal. By the time I was all done I had no money, but a lot of wood scaffolding and a piece of machinery that I had rented for a few days. During that time and weeks to come, I ate my fair share of ramen noodles.

I learned a very valuable lesson, one that not only bears repeating, but also may be the most important take away. When God wants to work in your life and has your full attention, He will give you the tools you need to do His work. Here is the thing you will need to remember: you must look to your left and then to your right. Everywhere you see a trash pile God sees a treasure chest.

He can use your trash to build a future for Him. That's right. There is deliverance and it most often comes from the debris we stare at in our lives each and every day.

It's sort of funny to think about now. I took the place of an entire crew. I went and finished off that house by myself and the next four homes after that.

This was in his newest subdivision, North College Park. Steve was not pleased with my work. The first complete home I rushed. I was so focused on just getting done that I had not put the pride and craftsmanship into it that Steve wanted me to have. He sat me down and told me that he thought that I had real potential and that he wanted to give me a chance because there was someone who had given him a second chance long ago. I had not heard that I had true potential before. I can honestly say it was the first time I remember hearing someone say that to me. Maybe you can think of someone in your life who needs to hear those words. It may make all the difference in the world!

I'm not sure why he decided to take a chance on me, but many years later I would ask Steve's wife, Lona Myrick, in preparation for this book. She told me that Steve thought I was smart and that I had a great deal of potential. He also said that if anyone was going to break the family curse, he thought it would be me. So I ask you as a reader, is there some family curse that you can break just by choosing to allow God to work in and through you?

He said that I was both ambitious and driven, but beyond all of those things Steve said that he saw something more...he saw a lot of himself in me. It blows my mind every time I think of this statement. I once heard Bishop T.D. Jakes say, "Powerful people recognize potential in people and people of potential recognize power when they see it."

Please don't take this the wrong way. Power is the power of God working through a person of His choosing, and the ability to see raw potential in people in and of itself is a gift from God. I will spend the rest of my life trying to help someone see his or her potential just as it was shown to me. This was one of the greatest gifts of grace ever bestowed on my heart. It is my honor to look for such raw potential in anyone I meet.

It was my guilt and my desire to make amends for what I had done to Steve that caused me to step up and take on that job by myself. It may have been "not letting Steve down" that caused me not to give up. I can tell there were many times I wanted to, but promise kept me from doing so. It was Steve's grace that gave me the opportunity and even though my work wasn't quite where Steve wanted it to be, he saw me take responsibility for my actions and he saw that I had the drive to improve myself, to grow, and to become not just a better employee, but a better person.

The next day, Steve took me out to a new site. Another job that he would give to my crew of one and on that day with a tool belt, handshake, and a heavenly whisper, Custom Home Exteriors was started. I did a house a week working fourteen-hour days, seven days a week. I struggled a great deal at first. I had no personal life of any kind, only work and a dream for four straight years. I have worked in the down pouring of rain, the dead of summer, and the 3-degree winters. I was the installer, warranty tech, billing, estimates, and most of all a child of God doing the best to honor my very special gift and this gift is called opportunity!

Soon, I was able to bring on a couple of guys to help and soon after that, a few more. It's been over fifteen years since that day and with God's blessing, my crew of one is now a corporation of 356 team members and subcontractors. Custom Home Exteriors is a special place. It is not one that focuses on siding, but instead on building people to help them where they are at, to decide where they want to go and to show them how to get there. We teach family. We teach culture. We make the most out of what we have at our disposal and no servant is above his master. That means the leader does not look down at his team, but rather looks at the army standing beside him to fight a battle in front of them all. It took one man, a handshake, and a God who would not give up on His child to make this very special place the many miracles it is today. Dave Ramsey said once, "Where there is not margin there is no ministry." We must learn to grow and fill our cup first before we can truly share with those around us. I am so blessed to have been able to help those who were just like me. They just needed an opportunity and God to show them what to do with it.

~~~~~~~

Guilt. I grappled with the guilt from walking out on Steve for over a year, but it ended up leading to one of the biggest blessings of my life. Should I have waited as long as I did to confront my guilt? Probably not, but the important thing to note is that it is never too late to make amends. You know, technically, I never asked Steve for forgiveness and, technically, he never told me that I was forgiven. But I showed my remorse in my actions and he showed me forgiveness in his grace. The building block for this principle is grace.

Grace (Worldview) - Grace is defined in *Webster's Dictionary* as an act of kindness, courtesy, or clemency. That's a pretty succinct and complete definition. It covers the dynamics of the type of grace that we can extend to others. Of course, grace from God goes a whole lot deeper, but that is something that we can explore when we get to the faith perspective. For now, I want to explore the importance in the grace that we show to each other. We have all experienced guilt, and I'm sure that each of us has probably had the unfortunate experience of not receiving forgiveness. Isn't it the most terrible feeling? It's even worse when that forgiveness we desire most comes from ourselves. I know when I spoke about forgiveness earlier in the book I said how important it was that you forgive yourself. Ultimately, because we have no control over other people's decisions, forgiving yourself is the most important step toward overcoming guilt. However, anyone who has ever been shown grace knows how much more fulfilling it is when you know that your trespasses have been forgiven. It seems to carry a little more weight because it moves beyond yourself and becomes a shared experience. It strengthens and grows all those involved both individually and collectively.

Action Steps for Learning to Operate in Grace:

1. **Forgive** – This is the most important aspect of grace. Forgive in love! We know that forgiveness is just as much about personal healing as it is reparation of a relationship. Remember your own feelings of guilt when dealing with others and be quick to forgive.

2. **Serve** – Learn to look for the ways in which you can help others. We all have needs but don't be afraid to look for the ways that you can really impact someone else's life.

3. **Speak life** – Yes, I stole this from one Mr. Toby Mac, but there is a profound truth in knowing how your words can affect others. Show grace in your communication and "*speak hope, speak love, and speak life!*"

4. **Show gratitude** – Operating in grace means being gracious. No-brainer, right? Go out of your way to show thanks and appreciation to others. Respond to grace with grace.

5. **Turn the other cheek** – This is most definitely the hardest one, but grace can sometimes have the biggest impact when it is undeserved. Maintaining a graceful

spirit is one of the best ways to overcome conflict!

Grace (Faith Perspective) – I've heard someone define grace from God as being given what we haven't earned. Isn't that the coolest thing about our God, His giving us His unconditional love despite our being undeserving? We don't have to earn salvation; it's free of charge. Amazing grace indeed! When that type of mercy and grace has been extended to you, how can you not glorify Him by extending it to others? Just as compassion is a huge tool in sharing Christ with others, extending grace is a tremendous way to let Him shine through you. However, though many Christians have accepted Christ, they are still overcome with guilt.

Please remember how you have been sanctified in Christ. Remember that there is no condemnation for those who remain in Him. Max Lucado says in *Grace for the Moment* that "when he says we're forgiven, let's unload the guilt. When he says we're valuable, let's believe him. When he says we're provided for, let's stop worrying. God's efforts are strongest when our efforts are useless".

But by the grace of God I am what I am, and his grace toward me was not in vain. On the contrary, I worked harder than any of them, though it was not I, but the grace of God that is with me.

1 Corinthians 15:10

Reflective Notes:

_____

_____

_____

_____

_____

_____

_____

_____

_____

_____

Journey Principle 9:
"Operate in Discernment, Not Deception"

Prayer

Father, thank you so much for seeking me to grow and mature. Please guide me in my purpose, plan, and help me to discern what is of you and what is not. Please lead me not unto temptation, but deliver me from evil. Lead me to green pastures and guide my path into your light. Help me to use my name in Jabez's place and trust you as you guide my mind and heart. In Jesus' name, amen.

Stephen Scoggins

Journey Principle 9:
"Operate in Discernment, Not Deception"

I had never felt more anxiety in my lifetime than the day that I left my home. I had been married for seven years and I had given absolutely everything that I could give, yet still found myself without answers. I spent so much time in prayer asking God for clarity on how to fix my marriage or, if it was His will, the strength to take the steps to move forward from the relationship.

The crazy thing is that my family and friends encouraged me not to follow through with the wedding. If I were truthful, I would say God urged me Himself. I thought I could make a difference in her life. Yes, the savior complex all over again. Some friends and family even went as far as to not attend the wedding. I never got any specifics, just that there were some signs of something not being right. There were symptoms of fighting for control and even abandonment issues, but like I said before, I truly thought I was meant to help her. We had been dating for almost two years and I can honestly say that I loved her. I hadn't seen any major breaks in integrity during our time together, only a couple instances that I chalked up to my own petty jealousy. Relationships are built on trust and girls are allowed to have friends that are guys. I didn't want to be the crazy boyfriend who didn't trust his girlfriend, but perhaps in hindsight, my feelings were more instinct and less paranoia. When I was growing up, I wanted a partner that I could trust fully and abundantly and I still believe this is what God intends for marriage.

We met in the winter of 2002 while I was working part-time at a gym. I had already started the business in 1998 that would lead to the freedom of writing this book, but each day I found myself with more energy than I had used. It's funny - I had noticed her and even run next to her on the treadmills a few times, but she had never given me a second look, not a glance, not a smile, until the day that I wore my *personal trainer* shirt and then she asked someone at the front desk, "Who is the new trainer?" I always found this funny because I had run beside her on the treadmill several times a few months earlier. So one has to ask, why did the impact of a trainer make a difference? I'm sure I will never know.

We began to chat off and on and a few months later we began dating. At first she was cute, encouraging, and witty. We did seem to click on most days. There were, on occasion, days when I was not sure how to take things she would do or say. I spent most of my time convincing myself it was more to do with my past wounds than her comments or actions. One day, I brought up the topic of marriage strictly out of curiosity. I was not ready for it just yet, but we had spent a lot of time together at that point. She replied that she did not see that in the cards because, and I quote, I was too "financially unstable." When she said this, I was somewhat taken back, only because I was busting my butt fourteen hours a day (building a business and paying off what was left of my over seventy thousand dollars of debt).

Some might consider that an obvious warning sign, but I didn't think there was anything wrong with her wanting some security. It obviously shouldn't be the only thing that she should be looking for, but I understood it being a factor.

At the time that we started dating, Custom Home Exteriors already had just over four years in business and started to develop a firm foundation and customer base, but as the business began to become more successful, I saw her interest in me begin to peak.

I had been working really hard for several years and the little free time I had I volunteered at the gym as a trainer. I did, however, find out after a few weeks that I was to be paid for my time. That was an unseen and nice surprise.

Things began to shift and soon she began to show interest in marriage and, more specifically, a ring. She even went as far as to describe the stone and band that she wanted and in no uncertain terms, said that she would not want anything less.

It was also about this time that I could begin to see the anxiety and fear in her life. Every time I went to visit her, she was like a different person. I know that the Jekyll and Hyde analogy is sort of overused, but it's applicable here. There were good days, and there were bad days, but to me it just seemed like she was hurting or that she had just had a bad day. I mean, everyone has bad days, right? And of course I thought that I could fix it. I wanted to help make it all better. This soon became my life, every day trying to appease, save, and manufacture happiness for her based on her demands. The favorite way that was used to control me was this comment "If you really loved me then..." I know enough now to know that is a controlling statement. It uses a perception of guilt to control and manufacture a certain environment and outcome. That's not love! That's control! Marital love is steeped in modeling Gods unconditional love. I've often struggle sharing parts of this story, because it took a long time for me to realize that controlling people often have had loved ones who controlled them. When she could not control the situation, she'd try and control something or someone else. She had a turbulent childhood and it's a wonder she made it through alive. I, unfortunately, mean she literally lived through it.

There were many things in her life that caused her great pain and out of respect for her and what she went through, I will not share those items here. It would not be fair in the least because we have all been through trials, betrayals, and things that have rocked our very souls and if not now, it will happen. The difficult part is knowing that all of these things drew me in closer. You see, I wanted to help, to believe in her, to help awaken her, and more than anything for her to know Jesus. I was asked in our close groups of friends why I tried so hard and I think it was because of grace. I knew as much as one person can know of another human and even witnessed first-hand things she struggled with. However, I got my boyfriend, fiancé, husband role confused with Jesus's salvation role.

I feel like I did at my core want to give her a *1 Corinthians 13* man. I did my best to love her in this way and based on friends and family, it was done to a fault. I think most believers are familiar with this scripture, but in essence when I apply this as a husband to a wife, this is how I would break it down: we, the husbands of the world are called by God to love our spouse in this way. Ephesians 5:25 says, "Men, love your wives as Christ loved the church and gave himself up to death for her."

So I personally believe 1 Corinthians 13 gives us an exact line of sight of what "true love" is.

True love is *patient.* Therefore, be patient and gain understanding of your wife; this includes her fears and her needs. God created her to be emotional, but with the emotion comes intuition. A godly woman's incites are powerful and God will give her warnings and understandings He does not give us as men because He wants to have relationships and real ones at that. The marriage covenant is supposed to mimic that of our relationship to God; it's supposed to be intimate and close.

Flash forward seven years into me trying to make it better: *"Lord, have I not sacrificed? Have I not committed? Have I not been faithful?"* This was one of the most painful things I had ever penned to paper, *"Lord, have I not provided to the best of my ability?"* The questions between God and I went on and on. I would pray daily, sometimes on an hour, for some answer, some resolution, but no clear answers ever came. They say that God always gives three answers: yes, no, and grow. Since I never got a clear yes or no, I assumed that I needed to grow. The problem, however, is that the more that I felt I was growing (some might distinguish between personal growth and growing in their faith, but to me they are one and the same), I would also find that I was growing further and further away from my wife and as a result, I was losing faith in my Lord. I can honestly say that both of these problems scared me to death.

We seemed to occupy the same space, but we were light years apart. It seemed no matter how hard I tried I could not gain traction.

In my mind, divorce wasn't an option. I knew what the Bible said about the sanctity of marriage and I truly believed that marriage was a lifelong commitment. I thought that as long as I remained faithful and accountable to God, at some point she and I would eventually get on the same page and that our marriage would be blessed. I prayed. I mean, I PRAYED!!! And then I prayed some more, begging, *"God, please fix me, fix her, fix us."* He had shown himself to me at the litter box (story coming later) but why was he not showing up now? I was far from a perfect husband, but I tried to remain attentive, compassionate, nurturing, and loving. I struggled greatly with the fact that she kept moving the bar up on me. If there were issues in our marriage I would confront them head-on, but it seemed like every time I overcame an obstacle, two more popped up in its place. I was beginning to realize that I was never going to be good enough, but I kept trying.

The promise that my wife and I had made to each other before God began to haunt me day and night, but I did not want to break God's heart nor the covenant of marriage. I believed in God's word and still do. I did not want to disobey the One who had carried me through so much. I didn't want to let Him down, but I felt like we had tried everything. I found myself slipping back into depression, not caring about anything except making it through the day. I couldn't see the extent of the depression, but friends and coworkers could see the changes. The happy, focused, and driven person they had met or had grown up with was no longer there. I was gone, checked out, and lost in apathy.

We were married almost right at seven years and for six of those years we had been in some form of marriage counseling. The first four years we relied on pastoral style counselors and the last two years we went all out with trained professionals. We actually seemed like we were making headway with our first professional counselor.

The marriage became more civil, moving from what seemed like enemies at times, always at each other's throats, to a more open communication level that even bordered on friendship. However, when we would go to counseling sessions, we would be given some sort of individual or joint task or exercise to do and I, being a list kind of guy, couldn't rest until I had crossed everything off of my list. My wife really seemed disinterested and wouldn't even attempt to do some of the exercises if she didn't feel like they would be helpful; unfortunately, this was nearly all of them. It's almost as if she felt she was above them which made me feel like she was above our relationship, that she shared no part in our troubles, and that something was wrong with me. It really felt like she was looking at me and saying, *'I hate you, but please don't leave me. I don't want to be alone.'* She would have fits of rage and then go completely docile. She would laugh and carry on and then start to cry for no apparent reason. And once again, our relationship began to grow stagnant.

Then one summer day I was getting out of the shower, and her cell phone kept ringing. It was a text message. This particular phone was a Nextel and the default settings were set to ring until the phone was opened and the message had been read. You know, the black and blue one with a silver center? It had the cool button at the top that made it pop open like a switchblade knife. I yelled to her to let her know that her phone was going off, but I guess she couldn't hear me all the way downstairs. I kept yelling, and the phone kept beeping. Finally, I hit the switchblade button and opened it to make it stop. My heart sank as I read the very brief and very painful message. It was a message from a former high school boyfriend that was making plans to come into town and was evidently coming back. The message read: *"So when is he leaving, it's been so long since I have seen you, I hope you can still recognize me LOL, I am looking forward to the hot tub, and I can't believe you still have that bikini from way back. Thank you for the picture, I can see that the years have treated you very well. Text me back and let me know when I should come over and say hi!"* (This is not too far off from the exact wording and for a very long time burned in my mind. To say I was shocked would be an understatement.)

While my instincts were screaming at me, I had no actual proof of infidelity, only proof that I wasn't being told the entire story. In that moment, I could not think of any reason why my spouse should be in , near, or around a hot tub with a former boyfriend, especially knowing I was going to be out of town on business on the dates they were talking about.

Honestly, it was pretty confusing for me because on the one hand, I could confront her and hopefully keep her from going down that path and potentially putting herself at risk to commit adultery or I could be really selfish, keep the text to myself, let her pursue whatever it was the message implied, and maybe I would finally have the "Biblical" grounds to move past this pain in my life.

I had been through so much torment that I was truly torn. As I sat there, all the memories of the things that my barbecue girl had done came rushing back and I became overwhelmed with emotion. I felt like the only honorable position I could take was to confront her and hopefully head this off at the pass both for her very soul and the chance for our marriage.

This man was still married to his wife as well so despite the hurt, despite the fact that I could possibly have a way out of the rollercoaster relationship, I heard God speaking to me as I sat on the bed crying and I knew what I had to do. I couldn't let her pursue this sinful path.

As I walked down the winding staircase of our home, my emotions circled from confused to angry, hurt, sad and back to confused. I knew that confronting her was the right thing to do, but it didn't make it any easier.

Standing there in front of her with the evidence in my hand, she denied everything! I can't necessarily say I was surprised and to be honest, I'm not even sure what I was expecting, but her blatant denial only made me angrier. What could I do? I only had a text message. I thought that nothing ever came of it until four years later when she finally admitted to having a very quick relationship with him. This, unfortunately, was not until after I had left the home that she began to tell me the truth and I guess it was the fear of me not coming back. Originally, all that time had passed and we were at another point in our relationship where it seemed like we were making headway. I was reminded of the Biblical story of Hosea whose wife, Gomer, left him for a life of adultery and then prostitution. Hosea had every reason to hate his wife and the Biblical grounds to move on, but he loved Gomer.

He loved her so much that when he found her for sale years later in a market, he not only purchased her freedom, but he took her back to his home and washed her feet. We have talked about the significance of washing feet with Jesus and His disciples. What an act of humility and compassion! I was somehow convicted of giving the anger of this trespass to God. I was obviously hurt, but I know that my God is a God of forgiveness, and I felt led to forgive her, too. I did not want to carry the baggage forward in our relationship or in my life for that matter. It wasn't the first time someone in my life had let me down and life experience teaches us that it wasn't going to be the last, but I had grown enough in my own journey that I wanted to operate in love and grace.

We moved forward. We started to work with a new counselor and things were starting to look up, or so I thought. We had not been intimate in over four years and were just shy of sleeping in separate rooms, but I was still trying to honor my commitment. Things changed when one morning, while getting ready for work, I saw her pour some vodka into her coffee. I was dumbfounded; it was like six am. I have clearly and openly discussed the effects of alcoholism in my family and a drink or two here or there was one thing, but liquor in your coffee in the morning was going to be an issue. I had to ask myself how long had this been going on. I was already feeling like I was *walking on eggshells* with her, never knowing when the smallest thing might set her off. Was it alcoholism or something more? I wasn't sure, but I decided not to confront her then and there and instead decided to bring it up in counseling. Bad move! Boy, I could see the fire burning in her eyes. The next few days after that session were interesting to say the least. She was yelling like I somehow had been snooping around the corner or something rather than downstairs making my normal protein shake before the gym.

A few weeks later, it was my wife's turn to go to her individual session, something each of us did with the therapist after a certain number of sessions together. As soon as her session was over I got a text saying, *"We are never going back there again. All she wants to do is break us up. She is saying there is no hope for us,"* she said, *"the therapist doesn't think that she can help us any longer and that we need to look for a specialist."* Did the therapist really say that? I had never seen that in her. If anything, the therapist had been very patient with the both of us.

I've got to be honest, at that moment I had pretty much

given up. I was emotionally and physically drained. I think that my wife could see it in my eyes when she finally made it home and she pleaded that we try one more therapist. I agreed. Here is the thing: she seemed to be lying to me directly. There was a glassy look in her eyes made of sheer terror and fear. I very reluctantly agreed, even saying this is my last ditch effort.

On the day that we arrived, I decided to be very candid about our relationship and explained to the new therapist that after two years of intense therapy and one, sometimes two sessions a week, I did not want to waste another two years starting from scratch. The therapist understood of my frustrations and asked that we give it six months and if we didn't see considerable progress then, it might be time for us to contemplate the alternative. The first three months actually gave me some hope. My wife was participating in the exercises and doing the assignments, but after month three it was like she flipped the switch off, and things went right back to the way they had been. I had finally reached my limit.

I believe that she had been unfaithful. I had no proof at the time, but I truly believed it. I knew that I had given everything, exhibiting patience through fits of rage and whirlwind emotions. I stuck by her side even though there were periods of what seemed like weeks at a time when I think she could not have cared less that I was even there. At this point, it had been almost four years since we had been intimate. And the kicker, to pacify her fear and anxiety toward bringing a child into this crazy world, I got a vasectomy even though having kids might be the biggest desire of my life! "As Christ loved the church," was what I kept telling myself. It sounds crazy doesn't it, that I made it even that long? I loved her and I really wanted to help her, but those feelings were all but gone.

The day was September 27; we had a counseling session that evening and followed it up with dinner at TGI Fridays. The night was just steeped in frustration. She was not trying to make progress with our therapy and she was flat-out lying to deflect any blame. I think the therapist saw right through. I carried the anger to dinner. When we sat down, I ordered water and she ordered a Long Island Iced Tea. I thought, 'No worries - one drink will be okay', but it was gone before we got our food. She ordered another...and then a third. She was in rare form, I must say.

When we got home, I let our dogs out and then started to carry the oldest one up the winding staircase because he had trouble walking the stairs on his own. She began nipping at my butt, which startled me a bit and, with the dog in my hands, almost made us fall backwards down the stairs. I gently swatted her hand from my behind to which she responded, "Oh, so now emotional abuse isn't enough. You're going to be like my stepfather and resort to physical abuse, too." I don't know how to describe how I felt. It was an inexplicable mix of disbelief and fury mixed with complete and utter sorrow. Me? Emotional abuse? Me? Physical abuse? The fury began to take over and I knew she could see it in my eyes, so she went and changed clothes, began crying, and then left the room.

Her crying was not like when people got their feelings hurt; oh no - this was wailing that could be heard down the street. This was the type of crying that would, in the past, get me to go and comfort her, promising her that everything would be okay. You see, the crying had become a game to her. She would wail until she heard me moving in her direction, then the wail would dwindle to a whimper, moving back to a wail if I stepped away again. I had finally had enough, lying speechless in the same spot that nearly four years earlier I had landed after reading the text message. I could not take the past pain, the new pain, or any future pain. I was done!

I packed a suitcase and left. Because of her crying she never heard me leave. It was over an hour before my phone rang and she pleaded for me to please come home. She cried hysterically, so much so that I called one of her friends to please go and check on her and make sure that she was okay. I just could not go back. I could not try to save her anymore. I had nothing left to give. I will admit at that moment, I did not know if I'd go back to her. I did, however, decide to sign an apartment lease for several months to try and get my personal stuff together and began going back to our first professional counselor to help deal with everything.

Over the next few months, I went to counseling by myself and learned a great deal. I dedicated myself to a new workout program to help relieve the stress and anxiety. I played hockey and even began writing this book. I moved forward. It wasn't easy. In fact, the separation and later divorce may have been the most difficult things that I have ever done in my life, but I knew that they were necessary. You see, ever since my spiritual awakening, I knew that God had called me to His purposes. He had a plan for me that involved living not in fear, but confidently pursuing the vision that He had given me.

I made her three promises as we went into our separation. I made this pledge for a six-month healing process for myself and to really determine for me what God wanted from me and I asked her to do the same. First, I would cover all of the household bills. My business had continued its success while we were dating and the foundations that had been laid before our meeting had turned into large oaks and continued its trajectory of growth while we were married.

I have been forced to deal with knowing I could have done so much more had I not been going through so much turmoil personally. A good friend once said it seems the business was blessed not because of my spousal relationship, but in spite of it.

I knew that she couldn't maintain the cost of living with only her income and I wanted to help. After all, I didn't hate her; I just knew the relationship was very unhealthy for both of us. If anything, I felt compassion for her pain and wanted to do right by her.

I would email her once a week just to check in and see how she was doing and check in on our two remaining dogs. I knew that we couldn't speak in person because of how emotional she would get and how unhealthy it was for my own personal healing at that time.

I wanted her to understand that even though it was time for us to separate for a time and contemplate moving forward with our lives, I respected her and my original commitment of marriage. I didn't see our separation as an opportunity to go meet other women. I saw it as a necessary step for personal health and growth.

My new-found strength and confidence scared her. Later, it became prevalent that the divorce was imminent. And while we were trying to have a dinner to discuss the future she confessed having had affair from a few years earlier. I honestly wanted to forgive her for this, but it was only part of the reason I chose not to reconcile. I think that it all started to become too real for her and I started to get replies to my emails that she was so sorry for all she had done and the pain that she had caused, that she was attending church regularly, going to counseling, and even that she was reconsidering having children. I wanted to believe her desperately, but it all just seemed a bit phony or rehearsed. In many ways, I felt as though she honestly believed what she was saying, but the moment I turned back her way it would be very different and worse than before. It also seemed like she tried to play on the three most important things in my life: *God, family, and integrity.*

I told her that I was happy that she was working so hard on herself, and trying to grow. I told her that I truly hoped that she learned to love herself. I wanted for her to find peace and happiness, but finally I made the choice that I was not going back.

After all, we had been in counseling for six years and she never tried. Why was she all of a sudden so concerned about losing me? Maybe she was just afraid to be alone or maybe it was because of the security that our relationship afforded her financially. I'm not sure, but I do know that the minute she finally realized that things were truly over, the true colors began to show. She became petty, vindictive, sneaky, and she began to take her own inventory of all of my financial assets. It really stunk because I wanted to believe that God was working in her life. I was blinded before, but now I realized that her "financially stable" comment years earlier was so much more telling than I had originally perceived. It made me wonder if she ever really loved me at all or if I was just the roommate who paid the bills, walked the dog, and mowed the grass. I had given and given and given some more and I finally noticed that all she did was take. What she didn't understand was that I wasn't out to get her. I didn't want to withhold anything from her. In fact, there was nothing I wanted more than to give her half of everything, wish her well and pray for her happiness. I just knew that happiness was not something that we were going to find together.

Unfortunately, she was relentlessly looking for anything that might help her get more and the person that I was now seeing made it all-too-clear that the last seven years of my life, all the pain, was a product of selfishness and deception.

Deception itself comes in many forms. In this story and area of my life, I was deceived by myself. I went into the relationship thinking that I was a knight in shining armor, that my love somehow could change a very damaged and wounded heart. I was then deceived by the outside areas of my life which came from my spouse. I set myself up to not be properly valued by the person I chose to marry. I put all my stock into trying to prove that if I could provide well, that I would be loved. I also found out how crazy exhausting that was. I set my own value up to be based on what I could give another and it's no wonder that I found myself *giving* to a *taker*. This, as you can see has been a very large challenge of my life, *giving* to *takers*. This has been a large work in progress, and has only been accomplished by trying to see myself how God sees me, by loving myself and by creating healthy boundaries. I am very happy to say that this part of my journey is leading me to much more fruitful relationships, friendships and areas where I, as a man, am valued very highly and not because of any one person, but rather because I know my Father in Heaven loves His son on Earth just as much as He loved His own personal beloved son. This is far more real when you or I realize that God sacrificed His son for the sons and daughters here on Earth. He knows the more we seek His relationship, the more intimate He can spend quality time with His child. God did not just say He loved us to show that this deception from evil was a lie. He showed us in action. The moment Christ breathed His first breath on this Earth until the moment He yelled *"'Father, into your hands I commit my spirit' and with this, he breathed his last."* [Luke 23:4]

Please understand that no one wants to be deceived. No one wants to be lied to or taken advantage of. I had given seven years of my life and perhaps my chance at ever being able to have children to someone who, I believe, became content in the lifestyle that I was able to provide for her. I also believe that there were other issues that played a factor in our relationship falling into disrepair, perhaps a borderline bipolar disorder, but I must state clearly that this is nothing more than my speculation based on research while in counseling. I am not a psychiatrist or psychologist. I can only speak from traits I have learned about while in counseling. Overall, it was beyond painful when I think about all that I gave and all that I gave up in order to express my commitment and devotion to the relationship.

Then, looking back, I have to ask myself what parts, if any, of our marriage was real? Was there anything that was true and tangible or was it all a lie? The truth is I learned a great deal about grace, mercy, and peace. These parts of the journey help me to understand how to both give it to others and accept it from my Heavenly Father and His son.

So, what is truth? What is truth to you? This is the quintessential question in life, is it not? I think that each of us, to some degree, seeks truth. It may be through faith and trusting in something bigger than this world and this life. For some it may be science defining and explaining the parameters of their existence. For others it's choosing to seek truth in their own personal reality by deciding on goals they feel are most important in life. They enrich those pursuits by creating meaningful relationships that bring joy into their lives. This is, of course, a generalization of the truth and the everyday pursuits of truth in personal and professional relationships and in our ordinary encounters and interaction, discernment helps us to operate in wisdom, deciding who we can and cannot trust. Discernment is the building block for this principle.

Discernment (Worldview) – Some people are just born with the gift of discernment while others spend a lifetime learning to discern. Trust isn't always easy to come by and unfortunately, the more you open yourself up to trust the more you also open yourself up to deception. Learning to discern takes time and practice, but it also takes heartbreak and sorrow. Some of life's biggest lessons come through pain while others come through mild inconveniences. The bigger ones might hurt a little more, but the little ones are the ones that can sneak up on you. How can you learn to discern? Open yourself up to experience life. Sure, this also opens you up to pain, but pain is one of life's great teachers. You must also accept the lesson. So many people experience deception, but they do not learn from the experience. Choose to grow and look for the knowledge you can take from your experiences and apply the wisdom in your future encounters.

Another important aspect to becoming a stronger discerner is also to learn from others' experiences. This isn't easy for everyone. A lot of us are like little kids whose parents tell them not to touch something that is hot, but we touch it anyway. We want to experience it for ourselves. This can make for an extremely slow maturation in discernment. Surround yourself with wisdom and soak it in. Learning from other's mistakes can save you a lot of pain and heartache.

Here are a few quotes that may help in different areas of discernment:

"When a person goes into a relationship emotionally needy, they are not going to have discernment in choosing people." -- Jennifer O'Neill

"We should not fret for what is past, nor should we be anxious about the future; men of discernment deal only with the present moment." -- Chanakya

"Just because something isn't a lie does not mean that it isn't deceptive. A liar knows that he is a liar, but one who speaks mere portions of truth in order to deceive is a craftsman of destruction." – Criss Jami

Discernment (Faith Perspective) – Deception is Satan's greatest tool and the Bible tells us that he uses deception in order to snare and trap us. God gives us the gift of discernment through His word and through the Spirit in order to be aware of and confront Satan's tactics. 1 Thessalonians 5:19-22 tells us, *"Do not quench the Spirit. Do not treat prophecies with contempt, but test them all; hold on to what is good, reject every kind of evil" (NIV).* Satan will not only attack with lies, but will come at you will half-truths disguised in prophecy. Learn to discern God's truth because Satan will disguise himself as a wolf in sheep's clothing.

If any of you lacks wisdom, let him ask God, who gives generously to all without reproach, and it will be given him.

James 1:5

Reflective Notes:

_____

_____

_____

_____

_____

_____

_____

_____

_____

_____

Journey Principle 10: "This Too Shall Pass and What Comes Next Will Be Greater"

Prayer

Father, please cleanse me of any doubts of my self-worth. Please help me to look back and see your fingerprints in the lessons my path has led me to learn. Clean me of my stumbling blocks. Show me that failure is never a person, but a lesson to grow from. Help me to know the truth behind "No eye has seen, no ear has heard, that which the Lord has for those that love him." (Paraphrase 1 Corinthians 2:9, NIV) Lord, in you I am no failure, but only a lump of clay you are molding, and I welcome your design! In Jesus' name, amen.

Stephen Scoggins

Journey Principle 10:
"This Too Shall Pass and What Comes Next Will Be Greater"

Failure tries to show itself in all shapes and sizes. It could be as small as your boss rejecting an idea or proposal at work to something as big as a failed startup or a marriage. Failure is tormenting no matter the size. Why? Because for many of us, and I would guess most of us, the first thing that we do when we don't succeed is to question ourselves. Somewhere along the way, we begin to see our failure as part of us instead of what it is truly meant for: a catapult for learning and growth. I have heard it said so many times that I am not sure who said the original quote "failure is not a person, it's an event". Sometimes, if we are honest, we can find fault in our plan, in our strategy, or maybe our commitment. Other times, we may have given absolutely everything, left it all on the field so-to-speak, and yet we still somehow managed to come up short. Either way, failure usually results in us asking one or both of these questions: *'What is wrong with me?'* or *'What have I done to deserve this?'* Have you ever asked yourself either one of those questions? I know I have; this is a whole book on learning from it. Of course you have and you are not alone (if you answered no we need to check you for alien DNA). Being introspective is just part of being human. We are hardwired to question. When we fail, it is natural to wonder why. The problem arises not in asking why we failed; it's in letting the reason for the failure define who we are or letting it create a fear that keeps us from trying again.

In this principle, we are not going to look at how to avoid failure. We are going to look at healthy ways to view, dissect, and learn from failure. Failure, just like every other obstacle in life, is another opportunity for you to grow. The greatest blessings in my life come from the treasure that God used in my trash or, in other words, the greatest blessings came from my greatest mistakes.

~~~~~~~

As I said earlier, suicide is a selfish act, but I have no choice but

125

to empathize with those who struggle with depression, self-esteem, and very dark thoughts. I am often told now of what my life looks like to those outside looking in. They have no idea what was faced in order to reach this point in my life and how Satan himself seemed to want to take me out.

In late 1997, I found myself sitting on that overpass in Raleigh, North Carolina. In 1997, I had gone from cocky, arrogant Stephen making great money to a virtually homeless military want-to-be. Some days, I am still in disbelief at my stubbornness. God had to humble me first so he could use me later. When I awoke that morning, I actually felt largely okay. I did not know that later that night I would make the choice to take my life. I wasn't thinking about my friends, family or any of the wonderful relationships with which God had blessed me. There was no highlight reel of memories playing before my eyes.

I mentioned that that day was not supposed to be just another day in the life of Stephen Scoggins; it was supposed to be the day that everything changed for the better. I had spent almost the last eight months training to go into the Navy and, hopefully, to become a SEAL.

Then, sitting in that small office with my hopes and dreams crushed, I felt like I was back at that moment, the moment where I was making a choice either to stay in high school or not. This choice was far larger. I had worked so hard to try to heal, try to grow, and try to not view the life before as one big failure. I wanted my life to have meaning. I wanted to help people. I wanted to be a kingdom builder.

I walked out of the MEPS office in a daze, oblivious to anything that was taking place around me. I could not comprehend what had just happened. I had failed. I had failed in school, I had failed at business, and now I had failed at getting into the military. I began walking and I began to hear a voice of less. The voice was so loud reminding me of everything I had done wrong, everything that I had failed at, and how little my life mattered.

When I reached that overpass, I crawled up the cement structure and took a seat on the metal tub-shaped railing. My senses were overwhelmed; there were tears in my eyes and utter uselessness in my heart. I was numb and all that I could taste was failure.

Then something changed. Everything became quiet. For the first time, I wasn't thinking of myself. Then there was a sound: the Spirit of Utterance, a still small voice that simply said, 'Stop. Be still.' Then something spoke to me and told me that there were people who were going to be affected by my decision. I needed to reach out to them and let them know what they had meant to me and that I would miss them. There was no true audible voice speaking to me. It was more like an urging, an impulse unseen, pushing me not off the overpass, but back into my Nike sneakers that laid quietly on the other side of the round rail and back into the relationships that were my only source of meaning. I remembered I had my old yellow screen 8" long Nokia 5160 cell phone with barely any minutes left. My 4'10" grandmother had given me just enough money to turn it back on so I could call the family once I arrived in Michigan, which was supposed to be my landing camp for boot camp.

I made a few phone calls, but there were no answers until I called Susan (Mamawama) and she answered.

Susan was the mother of a girl whom I had dated in high school. Her daughter Ashley was the first girlfriend that had taken my heart by storm and, as it turns out, I was Ashley's first boyfriend all together. The relationship had been over for a long while, but Susan, who had always treated me like a son while we were dating, still took care of me like I was her own. She clothed me, mentored me, and I knew she loved me. She knew something was wrong. She could hear it in my voice. She kept asking me where I was at and if everything was okay. I didn't know how to answer. I just cried. Finally, I told her that it was time for me to go and I said goodbye.

I said goodbye, but Susan didn't. She wouldn't say the words. She kept talking to me. I don't even know everything that she said, but she kept talking to me and when she was finished with what she had to say to me, she said my name until I answered her, "Stephen...Stephen?"

"Yes ma'am?" I replied. "Stephen, I want you to call me tomorrow morning at nine a.m." And then I knew that she knew and I cried some more. "Stephen! I want you to call me bright and early at nine a.m. tomorrow morning."

Susan was like a second mother to me. I take back the "like." In many ways, she was more a mother to me than my biological mother was able to be through much of my life. I had a tremendous love for her and a profound respect. I cannot say it enough. She treated me like I was her own, and I claimed her as mine. She walked me through my first real heartbreak when Ashley and I stopped seeing each other, telling me, "Stephen, this too shall pass and what comes next will be greater!" My answers to her requests had always been, *"Yes, ma'am!"* or truly, *"Yes, Mamawama!"* That day was no different. "Stephen, I want you to promise me that you will call me tomorrow morning. I'm going to be sitting by the phone waiting to hear from you. Do you understand?" "Yes ma'am. I promise. I will call you in the morning."

So then just before I hung up, she said these words again: *"Stephen, THIS too shall pass and what comes next will be greater."*

I hung up the phone with her prophetic words ringing in my ears. I just continued to sit there. What was probably a matter of minutes felt like hours, but I actually began to comprehend the promise that I had made. I'm not sure I even knew what I was saying while I was on the phone, but once it began sinking in, my love for Susan would not allow me to let her down. I can still hear her soft, somewhat raspy voice saying *"Stephen THIS to shall pass and what comes next will be greater."* I finally got a hold of my father, and he came and picked me up.

When I was preparing to leave for the military I had sold off all the possessions that I could and really everything I had to my name. I had even given away most of my clothes to Goodwill. I still had family that lived in the area, but I was virtually sleeping on my brother's couch, a friend's couch, and occasionally in a car. I was far too embarrassed to let them know I was largely homeless which to me means I was without a home or permanent shelter. Every single thing that I owned was inside of the duffle bag that was strapped across my shoulder. My world was unsteady and my mind was unstable.

After a few weeks of staying with random friends, I broke down and went back to my father's house with my tail between my legs. Talk about yet another layer of being humbled. I also had to go back to my brother who once idolized me, broken, penniless, and afraid. I really had no money for anything and my father had yet to get me back on Steve's framing crew from Principle 8. My brother did agree to give me fifty dollars to change out his litter box and I desperately needed the money. I remember the day very well. I was still very depressed, seeing only what seemed like shades of gray, red, and black. I had stayed on my father's couch the night before and walked the block over to my brother's. I walked up the large seven-step concrete stairs and unlocked the door. I walked in with the white walls to the left and right. The carpet was still the old beat up gray from when I had made the original purchase in late 1996. The house was - let's call it - "lived in" and he had told me he kept the litter box in the back bedroom. It was actually in the master bathroom. I could smell the overwhelming stench of cat urine and ammonia from the front door. I still had to walk past the blue wallpaper and lightly colored wood in the kitchen through the master bedroom door and then to the bathroom.

This might be the only light-hearted part of this story, but I walked through bedroom and finally through the master bathroom door and there it was: "The Litter Box." My brother had failed to mention that rather than cleaning it out every so often, they decided just to pour more sand on the top of it each time the litter box should have been emptied. It looked more like a mountain about twelve inches above the rim of the box with the rounded edges of an ice cream cone. It was truly nasty. It was peppered with tootsie rolls. I am sorry for the imagery, but it bears the acknowledgement of just how nasty this thing was. I can honestly say that if I had seen it first, I would have wanted more money, but let's just say God knows what He is doing!

One thing about me is I have always tried to keep my word. Sure, I have failed at it a few times, but it has always been at the forefront of my mind. So I knelt down, grabbed the scoop and plastic bags (yes, plural) and I started to scoop and scoop and scoop. Then suddenly, a snag! I tried even harder, but some the clumps had stuck together, and the weight of the clumped up lumps was too much for the scooper to handle and suddenly SNAP!! The scoop handle snapped off the scoop! To say I was frustrated was an understatement. Then, in order to get the job done, I was going to have to put my thumb up against the back side of the bucket part of the scooper, Ugh! This was so nasty, I could feel repressed rage building up inside me. I started to think to myself that this was what my life had come to, picking up cat crap with my almost bare hands. I began to scoop again and again. I could not wait to get this over with. So I began to scoop faster and faster, to just try and get the nastiness over with and then it happened! The corner of scoop scraped the edge of the bag and with one scoop the plastic bag tore and - you guessed it - the *blank* went everywhere and I do mean everywhere. That was it! I had had enough. I began to yell and fight with God at the top of my lungs. I can honestly say I didn't hold back. I am not sure if I was cursing, but my spirit was and it seemed like with every audible punch and kick I got weaker while He got stronger. To say I began to cry is so far from an understatement it's not even funny. Okay, I'll be honest. I began to sob and yell uncontrollably more and more.

Weeks earlier I had thought I was leaving to become a Navy SEAL and now I was paying for my basic needs by scooping cat crap. Could I be anymore of a failure? As I hovered over the toilet next to the litter box, I cried out to God. "Why are you punishing me?" I asked, "What have I ever done to deserve this?"

Have you ever felt that way? I am reminded of the story of Jacob in the Bible. Jacob had stolen his brother's birthright and had, in many ways, manipulated his way to what he thought was a true blessing only to find out that God wanted so much more from him. Like Jacob, I too was the rebellious son. I too had walked away from Him, and I too was brought face to face to wrestle with God. I challenge you to ask yourself right now if you are wrestling with God. Are you stuck trying to make sense of where your life is or where it has been? In the story of Jacob wrestling with God, the Lord had to only touch Jacob's hip socket in order to dislodge Jacob's hip from out of joint, yet Jacob continued to wrestle. He did so until the Bible says in Genesis 32:26 that "The man said, 'Let me go, for it is daybreak.' But Jacob replied, 'I will not let you go unless you bless me.'" Are you willing to fight with God all the way to the point where you hold on so tight to God that He has no choice but to see how badly you want a relationship with Him and how bad you crave not man's blessing but His?

The next thing God does is reply with this statement in Genesis 32:27: "The man asked him, 'What is your name?' 'Jacob,' he answered. Then the man said, 'Your name will no longer be Jacob, but Israel, because you have struggled with God and humans and have overcome.' Jacob said, 'Please tell me your name.' But he replied, 'Why do you ask my name?'

Then he blessed him there. So Jacob called the place Peniel,[b] saying, 'It is because I saw God face to face, and yet my life was spared.'"

As I shook my fist, I began to wrestle with my Creator. I slowly began to lose my once fiery streak and it turned from anger to sadness and from sadness to mourning! Yes, mourning. I mourned for every moment I had broken God's heart. I felt in my heart His presence for the first time since I was nine when my grandmother went to be with Him. I collapsed back on the toilet seat and continued to weep this time for His broken heart and just how badly He wanted me and had been pursuing me.

Unlike at the bridge where I only felt an urging, this time there seemed to be an audible voice which said in a quiet whisper, *"Leave her alone, and I will bless you."* Sounds random, right? Not really. I sort of left out the fact that due to my low state, I had searched for comfort with my old flame, my barbecue girl. I somehow related my self-value on my ability to attract love and attention from another person. What I was really searching for was a way to fill the empty shape in my heart, the special shape that is only created by the Divine. I had tried so many other things, except for the Creator's special shape, to fill the void in my heart. The things that you are thinking right now...justified. *"Leave her alone and I will bless you."* Concise. Straight forward. And I knew not to question, but to obey.

"*I will trust you,*" I answered. I believe in my heart I knew He was saying it wasn't the person as much as it was the focus. Loosely translated, turn away from the idol and turn toward Me and I will bless you. The great *I Am* had made me a promise.

I finally said, "*God if you are real, please I beg of you reveal yourself to me!*" In the quiet of crying and weeping I felt warmth over my body like a wave rushing of the rocks in a brook, and I said, "*Father, please forgive me. I'm sorry. Please help me. I love you. I need you. Please hold me. I am so wretched, and I have no idea what I have been doing, and I don't know where I am going. I only know I want to go where You are!*"

The amount of overwhelming comfort, warmth, love, and peace I felt was indescribable, but I knew it was real. At that moment, I was His and He was mine. It was at that moment that I finally understood what Zig Ziglar had always said: "I know who I am and whose I am. "

There is not a person on Earth that can convince me God the Father is not real or that His son, Jesus, did not walk this Earth. Jesus died for me so I could live for Him and for the rest of my life I will. He suffered utter and complete abandonment from the Father on the cross so I may never feel abandoned again.

It was a few short years before that I had realized the correlation between Jacob and I. I realized that God the Father often calls many of his children by getting them stripped of things that encumber Him from being seen. He will then get them alone in His presence. He will then wrestle with us on our sin, our pride, and our relationship with Him and our purpose and then He reveals himself in a very mighty way. I first needed to be stripped of everything I placed enormous value in, all the things that I was chasing that were not of Him and prevented me from seeing Him. He then took me to look square at my sin, to help me understand it was, in fact, present in my life. It was shown to me in the form of a very full litter box, full of stench and the excrement of life. The moment He helped me realize my sin and my need for Him, the wrestling started.

So many times when I look back of the story of Jacob wrestling with God and look back at my own journey and wrestling, I see not a God, but a Father that truly loved me and through a great deal of patience and understanding, allowed me to see the fullness of my personal litter box. He showed me my absolute need for him. You see, I believe the reason the handle broke on the scooper and then without fail the bag broke was because I was never meant to empty the litter box of my life. Jesus died to empty my litter box and then arose on the third day so it could be cast to the furthest sea never to be seen or remembered again.

Do you get focused on doing things on your own? Do you constantly struggle with the right or the wrong in life? Do you live in the land of "what ifs"? Do you only see confusion?

If this is you, then, my friend, you are struggling with God the Father. If you want clarity, purpose and design, then bear down and lean into Him and don't let go until the blessing is yours. He will give you a new name in the Book of Life.

The Father never puts you in as you are, but rather puts you in as He now sees you. He calls you not wretched sinner, but gives you the name of son or daughter. He wants to make you a mighty new creation, full of life and fervor! The Father may have to touch your hip and dislocate a few things in your life in order to prepare your path and your journey. I encourage you to welcome the cleaning of your life from the inside out. This is part of the sanctification we mentioned earlier. It is a process. The process is the certainty that the Father is there with you. With the Father, quality growth always comes with the process. You see when you lean into the Father, He leans into you. Just as a child reaches for his father, the father opens his arms for the warm and caring embrace of the child he so desperately loves. What will be your moment? When will you decide to reach out? Once you have an encounter with the Father, you will see.

It was in that moment that I realized my life was about something bigger, something more. While I had failed, I was not a failure. My journey, the experiences that had brought me to the lowest of lows, were the moments that would mold and shape me and help me to become the man that I was supposed to be. I hadn't failed. I had been stretched. I had grown. I had been tempered in the flames of adversity. What changed? I believe it began with my willingness to be obedient to my God, my Father and to finally look at myself the way He looked at me. This can make all the difference in your life. I will continue to encourage that your focus should not be on this world alone, but while you are on this Earth, you can experience contentment, happiness, and peace just by altering your approach. Knowing who you are and what you want to achieve and to persevere, no matter the size of the obstacle placed in your path. Every great oak tree begins with the smallest of acorns.

Maya Angelou said, *"You may encounter many defeats, but you must not be defeated. In fact, it may be necessary to encounter the defeats, so you can know who you are, what you can rise from, how you can still come out of it."*

Perseverance isn't about sheer will; it is a teaching tool that helps us better understand who we are by showing us the things in which we are willing to fight and sacrifice to obtain or achieve. Perseverance speaks to your identity because it makes clear the things in life that are important to you. Perseverance is our building block for this principle.

I have experienced the need for perseverance in my life. I have dedicated time to colleges and universities that encourage high school dropouts to pursue their GEDs. I have volunteered and had the privilege of speaking at Step Up Ministries, a local program that inspires and provides opportunities for those that have been in prison, those in need of skilled labor training, and those who are reintegrating themselves into society. Because I founded and run my own business, I have read numerous books, studied the curriculums, and attended countless seminars on the topic of business, leadership, and personal growth.

Below is a list of the characteristics that I believe separate those who persevere and exhibit resolve from those who give into the fear of failure. While I have separated the worldview and the faith perspective in the previous principles, I will explore the differences for each characteristic as is applicable in the characteristics that are discussed.

Action Steps for Perseverance:

1. **Engaging the moment** – Living a life of perseverance is not simply saying, *"C'est la vie."* It is not a mere acceptance of circumstance, but the application of experience. You should use your life lessons to help shape your ideology, morals, ethics, and how you take action in the world. Accepting the lessons of the past helps to overcome the fear of failure and allows you to concentrate on the here and now. While you should use this wisdom to experience the present, trusting in perseverance will also allow you to overcome the unpredictable roads ahead.

   From a faith perspective, I think it's important to remember how precious our time one Earth is. James 4:14 says, *"Why, you do not even know what will happen tomorrow. What is your life? You are a mist that appears for a little while and then vanishes."* Honor the Father by living life fully. Don't look back with regret and wonder what more you could have done to advance His kingdom.

2. **Accepting change** – C.S. Lewis is quoted as saying "to be in time, means to change." It is a part of life. It is inevitable. From what I have observed of those who seem to exhibit strength in perseverance, it almost seems like change is welcome. Maybe they just have a better understanding that growth accompanies change. Maybe, from their point-of-view, living a life without challenges isn't living at all. Whatever the reason, the people that I consider to be mentally tough are also the ones who are most willing to step out of their comfort zone. Coincidence? Absolutely not.

   For the believer, I think that one of the first steps to accepting Christ is admitting that you are broken and missing a piece of yourself without the King of Kings. With that recognition should bring about the desire to change. Don't ever let that process become stagnant. Don't ever shy away from letting God stretch you and teach you. As you grow closer to Him, trusting more and fearing less, earnestly seek the ways that He would call you onward and upward.

135

3. **Take responsibility** – John Burroughs said, "A man can fail many times, but he isn't a failure until he begins to blame somebody else." Wow! I don't need to add much more to that. Persevering means taking responsibility for your failures. Don't shift the blame to others, but look for the ways in which you could have done better. Learn, grow, but at the same time learn to recognize when things were outside of your control and don't beat yourself up over the things that you could not change.

4. **Learn from your mistakes** – I believe the quote that "Insanity is doing the same thing over and over and expecting different results," is attributed to Albert Einstein. While that's obviously not the technical definition of insanity, the quote does ring with some truth. I think we all have that friend or acquaintance that just seems to keep screwing up in the same ways time and time again. That's the exact opposite of perseverance! Persevering isn't just pushing forward; it's moving forward with accumulated and calculated wisdom. It's digging through the trash of past mistakes and developing the treasure of your future!

5. **Never give up** – Okay, so this is kind of an obvious aspect of perseverance, but I grew up in Raleigh, North Carolina where Jim Valvano's *"Don't give up...don't ever give up,"* inspired many long before the V Foundation had the global recognition it has today. I think that it is important to remember that perseverance doesn't just mean pushing forward after failure. Perseverance also means pushing through adversity. Be tenacious. Obstacles threaten most successes and the great achievements in this life are great because of what was overcome to claim triumph. Push forward, keep your head up, and never, ever give up. Galatians 6:9 tells us, "Let us not become weary in doing good, for at the proper time we will reap a harvest if we do not give up."

The most encouraging journey principle is there is a heavenly Father. This Father wants nothing but the best for you. His purposes and ways are not like ours and often do not make sense, but they are always better than we ever hoped for and ever could imagine. It takes a desire to be obedient.

My friend and one of my mentors, Chris LoCurto, mentioned to me once, "When God's word says in Psalm 37:4, 'Delight yourself in the LORD, and he will give you the desires of your heart.' He is not saying that He will indeed give you everything you have ever wanted. He is saying as you learn to know and obey me, your heart's desires will change and align with mine. When our desires align with God's, He does not just stop with the realization of those dreams. He adds an added measure to your life. Just like in Luke 6:38."

Life's journey is more about who you become, who you inspire and how you give. If you give large, you will be given large. Set out to create a legacy. Legacy thinking says I am making decisions, action, and giving to support the betterment of all mankind. Life's journey is about how to get back to the One with whom we were separated from due to sin in the world. I have found that God the Father will give you all the inspiration and wisdom you will ever need. His wisdom is always taught and never caught. When we understand the purpose behind the pain, our struggles begin to resemble a pregnancy bringing in new life into the world. There is always a pulling, a stretching and even at times immense pain in birth, but it always leads to new life.

We have talked a lot about the principles that have helped me design, adapt, and grow on my journey, but none of this matters unless you take action on your own journey. There are principles that He has locked inside of you. These principles will not only help you, but are universal secrets waiting to be communicated to the world through the simple acts of your life's journey.

"Give, and it will be given to you. A large quantity, pressed together, shaken down, and running over will be put into your lap, because you'll be evaluated by the same standard with which you evaluate others."

Luke 6:38

Reflective Notes:

_____

_____

_____

_____

_____

_____

_____

_____

_____

_____

The Parable of the Lost Son[8]

11 "Jesus continued: "There was a man who had two sons. 12 The younger one said to his father, 'Father, give me my share of the estate.' So he divided his property between them."

13 "Not long after that, the younger son got together all he had, set off for a distant country and there squandered his wealth in wild living. 14 After he had spent everything, there was a severe famine in that whole country, and he began to be in need. 15 So he went and hired himself out to a citizen of that country, who sent him to his fields to feed pigs. 16 He longed to fill his stomach with the pods that the pigs were eating, but no one gave him anything."

17 "When he came to his senses, he said, 'How many of my father's hired servants have food to spare, and here I am starving to death! 18 I will set out and go back to my father and say to him: Father, I have sinned against heaven and against you. 19 I am no longer worthy to be called your son; make me like one of your hired servants.' 20 So he got up and went to his father."

"But while he was still a long way off, his father saw him and was filled with compassion for him; he ran to his son, threw his arms around him and kissed him."

21 "The son said to him, 'Father, I have sinned against heaven and against you. I am no longer worthy to be called your son."

22 "But the father said to his servants, 'Quick! Bring the best robe and put it on him. Put a ring on his finger and sandals on his feet. 23 Bring the fattened calf and kill it. Let's have a feast and celebrate. 24 For this son of mine was dead and is alive again; he was lost and is found.' So they began to celebrate."

---

[8] NIV, www.biblegateway.com

Epilogue

"A DEDICATION TO MY PARENTS"

Prayer

"Oh, glorious God, that you would bless each reader indeed and enlarge each of their territories! Let your hand be with them and keep each of them from harm so that they will find healing instead of pain." Dear Lord, please help us to become healthy, wealthy and wise in Jesus' name amen."

Stephen Scoggins

"Honor your father and your mother, so that you may live long in the land the LORD your God is giving you."

Exodus 20:12 NIV

I am blessed and honored to introduce to you my father Glenn Scoggins and mother Donna Stallings. My family (as I shared with you earlier) has had some healing to do. My parents are gracious enough to allow me to share their journeys with all of you. And after prayer and discussion we decided it would be helpful if they told their personal journeys in their words. In this epilogue, my parents and I want to show how families heal all things through and with God.

Glenn and Donna will share with you the challenging adversities in their lives and how they took those adversities and turned their lives around through the grace and glory of God.

I am so incredibly proud of them. I honor their strength as well as their vulnerability and honesty. My family are proof that the only way to heal others in a grand way is to heal yourself first, by applying God's Principles. My parents made conscious decisions to fight their way back. They both felt defeated and felt like there was little to no hope. They decided that their adversity would be a catapult.

The only person who never makes it back is the one who does not take the first step, followed by the second. The journey always starts with the first step. Hope is built on the foundational choice to share testimony that encourages others. My parents have been working hard to heal, deal, and make better choices. As a result of their commitment to take the first step (the next step and the next step), they have become fantastic grandparents and great parents to myself and my brother Ryan.

Glenn and Donna both have diligently looked for ways to strengthen their relationship with my brother and me. My mother has become a great encourager, friend and supporter to her children's lives. She is a giver. My father does not miss a single one of my "adult league" hockey games. What makes this even more powerful is that many of these games don't start until after 10pm at night.

We want to share with you how families heal together. We pray these testimonies teach the power of healing yourselves first. By healing yourself first, you offer others the chance at life, joy and happiness. It is true we all fall short, and we all stumble at times, but when we offer grace to others, it somehow pours grace into our lives.

We should always seek first to understand, gain perspective and then relate to those who have been hurt or are hurting. You may just find out like I did that with every Journey the principles followed in life lead us closer or further from our passions, dreams, and God Himself. Seeking to understand yourself fully and completely is the first step to your healing. I believe we all need a new hope, a new healing, and a clear purpose. We all need God.

"For I know the plans I have for you," declares the LORD, *"plans to prosper you and not to harm you, plans to give you hope and a future. Then you will call on me and come and pray to me, and I will listen to you. You will seek me and find me when you seek me with all your heart. I will be found by you," declares the* LORD, *"and will bring you back from captivity.*

Jeremiah 29:11-14 NIV

MY MOTHER DONNA STALLINGS PERSONAL TESTIMONY

It is my hope and prayer by sharing my testimony that others may be touched and healed. God, bless the brave who are willing to start their journey back to you. It is worth every second and moment.

My childhood was very dysfunctional. I was very young when my parents divorced and was thrust into a world of uncertainty. I was never afforded the luxury of just being able to be a child. I had to grow up very fast and deal with things that no child should have to experience.

I loved my mother very much and wanted to please her, but I always felt like I fell short of her expectations. I did not realize it at the time, but my Mother was a hurting woman, and as previously stated "hurt people, hurt people." I believe this is a cycle of bullying. I have heard Stephen mention that when others can't control themselves, they seek to control others, and a way to control others, is by hurting them. I was repeatedly told I was worthless, and if you are told something long enough - you begin to believe it and so I carried the belief I was unworthy in my heart for a very long time. I always felt alone and never felt like I had a soft place to fall. I learned early, to be very distrustful and leery of people.

My mother remarried a couple of times to very abusive men. I remember laying in my bed at night hearing the beatings she endured at the hands of these men, wondering if I was next. I was so scared, and I didn't know how to protect her. I remember being yanked out of my bed in the cold of the night in just my nightgown to run and call the police.

The only relief that I had was when my mother would send me to visit my father during the summer. This, unfortunately, opened up a whole new can of worms for me. My father had remarried and had four children from his second marriage. Even though I loved my father, brothers and sister dearly, I felt jealous and pretty much felt like an outcast. I felt lost in turmoil, and it seemed unfair that others in my family could move on with their lives. There was a lot of resentment between my father's new wife and me. She resented me, and I resented her too. I felt like she took my Daddy away from me, and I guess I was a reminder of a past marriage. My life always seemed to be filled full of pain, hurt, and resentment.

I just felt lost.

When I grew older the only thing I wanted to do, was get out from under my mother's instability. I wanted to escape and try to start my life on my own; promising myself that I could and would do better. I soon met my children's father and rushed into a marriage. At the time, I thought I was in love, and everything would be alright. But like so many women, I fell into the trap of thinking I could change him. Why did I feel I needed or wanted to? My husband was an alcoholic, but I still tried. I was lied to, cheated on and betrayed by a man who professed to love me. Looking back, I am not sure I ever saw stability in men with the exception of my father. My mother's men didn't pan out, and a man I hoped would love and cherish me didn't either. I can't say everything was all bad - because out of the marriage my children were born. I can truthfully say that Stephen and Ryan have been the greatest blessings in my life. Even with that being said, I will admit that no matter how hard I tried I still felt like I fell short of being the mother that I should have or could have been.

I have asked my children's forgiveness for my shortcomings, and I know I have expressed that I love them very much and always have. The scriptures have taught me that all have fallen short of the glory of God, and not one is without blemish, not one. I learned each day to trust Jesus more and more. He is my rock and my fortress, and as I act on his principles, I seek my restoration in him and through him. In life, I have learned that we all make mistakes, and we should take full responsibility for them. Truthfully, it wasn't until I became a born again Christian and washed in the blood of the Lamb that I knew without a shadow of a doubt that I had been forgiven of all my past sins. Jesus Christ loves me no matter what. He died so that I might have everlasting life. He also died so that I might enjoy each new day with his peace, grace, and mercy. I don't have to be afraid anymore or believe the lies (false evidence) used to keep me feeling unworthy. He has made me realize that I do have great value and that I am worthy of being loved. There are times where I still have struggles, but I know that all I have to do is take it to the Lord in prayer. He is faithful and forgives, guides and offers grace. It is his grace that sustains me and guides me each day to a more fruitful happier life.

May my story be a light for anyone who has struggled in a similar ways.

May God richly bless your Journey!

Donna Stallings

"Look at the birds of the air; they do not sow or reap or store away in barns, and yet your heavenly Father feeds them. Are you not much more valuable than they? Can any one of you by worrying add a single hour to your life? And why do you worry about clothes? See how the flowers of the field grow. They do not labor or spin. Yet I tell you that not even Solomon in his entire splendor was dressed like one of these. If that is how God clothes the grass of the field, which is here today and tomorrow, is thrown into the fire, will he not much more clothe you—you of little faith?"

Matthew 6:26-30: NIV

MY FATHER GLENN SCOGGINS PERSONAL TESTIMONY

My family and I were raised in the Church. I was first saved as a teenager (14 or so). I always struggled with the hypocrisy of the leadership that I watched in the church we were attending.

My father's handshake was as good as gold. His word was his word! He was such a strong man. He would have to be - to survive the bombing of Pearl Harbor (this was long before PTSD was a topic). My father struggled with alcohol for years and finally began his journey to sobriety, around the time we started attending church. (I mentioned it already but my father Joe Scoggins (ox) had witnessed horrors at the bombing of Pearl Harbor. He had done the unthinkable and survived as 2500 of his brothers died and over a thousand more were wounded in the bombing. He would often say; it happened so fast that they were only able to get one round off before it was over.)

It was not long before he had made serious headway and had been sober for a long time. One weekend a few of his fellow deacons asked if he wanted to join them on a fishing trip. Somehow while they were out fishing - the decision was made, and my father had his first drink with them, and then another.

A few Sundays later we were attending church when my father stood before his peers and acknowledged that he had fallen off the wagon (so to speak). My family, and I watched as my father stood broken hearted as his deacon brothers looked on not saying a word of their influence or decision to drink with him over that weekend. I watched my father who always strived for integrity no matter what the shortcomings, stand up in front a crowd embarrassed and ashamed before God. My father was not perfect, but his handshake meant something and as a man of integrity he felt he could not stand up and lead. He chose to step down as a deacon as the onlookers - looked on.

My father's heart was broken and the fact that the others did not stand with my father while being accountable for their choices too, made the place smell of hypocrisy. I have to admit that influenced my life in a negative way, the God I once loved, I began to feel distant from. I was angry with the other deacons for not even so much as supporting my father in that instance.

I think like most any journey, when we start to walk away from God and live by other means we almost instinctively give the devil a foothold to get started. I had not completely found my identity just yet and more than anything just wanted to be accepted and "cool" if you will. I started putting a lot of effort into being "cool" smoking, drinking, etc.

I one day woke up, and there was such a hold on my life that it didn't take long before I was an alcoholic (before I was 20). I grew up working with my brothers and my father in the construction trade and continued to struggle with the new force of alcohol in my life. It was not apparent to me at first. I met a woman I was very attracted to, and later we married at my tender age of twenty-three. I still did not fully know who I was at that point and struggled with my identity to a certain extent. I tried to be solid and be a man like I believed my father was. I first became a father at twenty-six with the birth of Stephen. I always thought I was pretty good at being a dad. I loved my children but never realized how my alcohol affected my marriage, my children or myself for that matter.

My life continued to show signs of turmoil off and on for years. I was still not ready to talk to God, or accept the feelings from my childhood. I never dealt with being so angry with God and those hypocrites that hurt my father. I intentionally stayed away from church for many years.

My journey had finally led me to a clearer place in my life. While at a St Patrick's Day event, I took my last drink and never went back. This may be fitting since my son Ryan's middle name was Patrick. I had reached sobriety almost a full fifteen years with what might have been my first encounter with God in a long while. I had quit smoking and began to move forward clearer than ever before.

I was still struggling with how my decisions around drinking had led to other transgressions. I would ask myself how God could love me after all the mishaps and bad decisions. Ryan and Stephen both would assure me that God loved me and was not going to give up on me. It was in the late 90's both of my boys, Ryan and Stephen began to attend church regularly. Ironically it was the same church they attended during the time they stayed with their grandmother earlier in their childhood.

Their grandmother would send them on a local church bus as it came on Sundays, when they were younger. Ryan and Stephen invited me to go to church with them one Sunday, and I did.

So many times before I had listened to Satan, who told me I would always feel this way. I had stopped drinking almost 15 years before this point, but even that was never enough. On about the third trip to church with the boys, I began to realize that the life I had been living for the last 20 years, could be and would be forgiven. I was sitting with both of my sons (in whom I love so much), and I told them with tears in my eyes, I was ready. Together we made the journey back to the Lord, and I am never looking back. That day I rededicated my life for Christ and have spent the last ten years taking each step based on his principles for living. I can honestly say life has been better than it has been in a very long time. My boys are back together as brothers, and I make a great grandfather. In my heart, I am proud of the Christian men my sons have become. I realize I am still a "work in progress" but I think we all are. One thing for sure is with each mistake comes a better principle and with every principle, there is further love and redemption through Christ.

Though I get mad at myself when I make a mistake here or there, I have finally learned the principle of perseverance and no longer let these things stop me from picking myself up and trying again. I work hard where I can to serve others now, and my life is no longer all about me or the guilt I placed on myself for over two decades.

I pray I can just let you know - if you struggle with the things I did, then you know what the Devil says when he lies to you. How convincing he can be in telling you that a drinking man will always be that way, and you have gone too far in order to be saved.

I am the living proof that the Devil is a liar and Christ is king and has risen. He saved me and taught me a new way, through his principles. Jesus loves you, just as he loves me. It's true it's very hard to understand another's pain without first experiencing the kind of problems we faced until they have walked in the same shoes.

I pray to God every day that he will just hold me close and keep me in his will. The Devil tries now and then to say it again, but God tells me every time "The Devil is a liar" and I now have a savior I can trust. I have living proof that Christ is real, and God answers prayers.

I realize I had struggled for many years, and even though I had left the church for so many years, I never blamed my problems with the church on God. I could not help that on the day that each of boys were born I prayed to God to not let them struggle with the things I struggled with and to hold them and keep them close. My God, my savior answered those prayers in an abundance that I cannot describe. Not only did the Father answer that prayer they both have become great servants of God. Each new day God renews his promise to hold me close and keep evil away. Each day I thank him for all the years before and all the new year's he restored. If you have ever struggled with the things, I have spoken of. Just know Christ is King, and he will meet you where you are and grab your hand, and literally walk you step by step out of the darkness. He will never leave you or forsake you. I was once lost, but now I am found, and his love knows no bounds. I hope you enjoyed the book; my sons are very special men to me. God Bless you and may your Journey lead to peace. This is the first time I have shared my testimony, and I pray it makes all the difference to someone.

God Bless!
Glenn Scoggins

My Journey, God's Principles made all the difference in my life, I once was lost but now I am found, I was once blinded in darkness but now I see.

Stephen Scoggins

YOU ARE THE RIPPLE EFFECT

Here is the secret. This Journey was never about me; *it was always about you.* You're a pebble, and your ripple can affect another person's decision to heal. This is how one life can affect another.

We are all pebbles in the hand of God. He has many oceans of living water and with each newly healed pebble, He can make waves of joy for others. When we choose to make the decision to follow His Principles, He knows He can trust each one of us with His purpose. He then casts these glorious pebbles into the living water in His heavenly streams.

We are the rock that builds his church. Every single soul that chooses to believe in His promise of redemption, and acknowledges He has a purpose and are willing to be guided by God's Principles can create ripples that affect the eternity of others. It is knowledge of growing from our experiences, growing from our adversity's to be a beacon of light to those who are still lost in darkness.

Your voice matters to the kingdom, your heart matters to the kingdom, and your faith in the Father matters. *"Nothing screams louder than a repentant believer willing to share their testimony in front of those that need healing and deliverance from the darkness."* When we believe in his principle, and our light is cast out into the darkness, our voices are amplified louder than any concert speaker. God's voice that called out to the darkness and said "Let there be light" and there was light, and he called it good. Your voice can be that light, it *"will"* be the healing to someone else's needs, and the grace never offered and the peace never felt.

You are that voice you are God's tool to "Let there be light" and *you* will be that light. You can be that light if you will choose to grow in his principles each and every day. You and I are warriors, and it's time to heal and get back to the battle. I hope The Journey Principles has offered information, new hope and a new future to you. Your life matters, it matters to you and every soul you lock eyes with. Your decision, to grow from adversity, is precisely the light you can offer others.

Thank you again for taking this journey with me, and I sincerely hope you have enjoyed this writing and seek to make a difference in the lives of others.

For more information, please visit, www.stephenscoggins.com there you will find we add new information and programs to aid in your growth, prosperity, walk with God and daily living. You can also follow us on Facebook, Twitter and sign-up for our weekly newsletter.

Sincerely,
Stephen Scoggins

YOUR JOURNEY, GOD'S PRINCIPLES

ALSO FROM JOURNEY PRINCIPLES™ LLC

The Journey Principles
10 Simple Principles for a Life Journey that Matters

The Journey Principles
Putting Principles into Practice
Course Workbook

Thrive to be The Real Deal
Youth Motivational Program

The Journey Principles
10 Business Wellness Secrets for Entrepreneurs

The Journey Principles
There is No Lack of Gain
1 CORINTHIANS MAN
His Love, Her Respect

The Journey Principles
There is No Lack of Gain
1 CORINTHIANS WOMAN
Her Love, His Respect

The Journey Principles of Restoration
Daily Devotional 2016

The Journey Principles Reader Reviews:

"Stephen's words gave me so much more than hope; they gave me a new sense of courage to break through the pain in my relationship and use it to grow. I read the principles whenever I need a reminder of how to be present and get through the day ahead."

-Amber Muse

"I just finished Stephen's book. I'm going through my own journey and this book was great. It helped put all my emotions, feelings and thoughts into perspective. Thanks Stephen for sharing your story."

-Chris

"The Journey Principles is a very inspirational autobiographical book written by Stephen Scoggins. Mr. Scoggins draws upon his life experiences to illustrate his guiding principles that lead towards a fulfilling and rewarding life. A must-read!"

-John

"Stephen, your heart actions have been so motivating to me that I am doing things these dates that a few months ago I would have never even considered! I do things even if I am afraid of failure, or rejection, and so far ALL of my fears have been for naught and every small step I took out of my comfort zone has a resulted in LEAPS of progress for me and the people I have reached out to and for!!! What a blessing!!"

-Laurie Yaw Quote

"I'm very proud of you and your accomplishments and what you'll continue to do in the future. With Karen by your side there is nothing you won't be able to do. I think God has brought the two of you together at just the right time. The Navy Seal loss is our big gain...and we are so looking forward to having you in our family...We will continue to support you in any direction you choose to take."

-Mom Salley

"Demonstrating both vulnerability and insight, Stephen Scoggins uses his personal joys and trials to show the miraculous nature of God's work in his life. In his book The Journey Principles, Scoggins weaves accounts of his past with his insight into topics like spirituality, relationships, and success, creating a unique blend of equal parts memoir and motivation. The Journey Principles is a great resource for those interested in a more spiritual approach to the struggles we all face in life. Because of his unique background, Scoggins tackles difficult topics in an intimate way that feels very accessible to the reader. "

-Madison Carr

"An autobiographical book that's full of inspiration and wisdom, "The Journey Principles" is a great example of turning the tragedies in life into triumphs. Filled with a multitude of examples from his own life, Stephen Scoggins shares his journey as a growing Christian."

-Rebecca Henderson

This book is amazing. What says he is so true and hits home with me. I have to stop reading so I can take time to absorb what he says and commit it to memory. I have just begun to read this and need to say how much I love this book!

I am a worrier and even through the grief of losing my Mom last month I am hearing his words resound in my mind with such truth from God. Words that will help me defeat my unreal fear and anxiety. I "worried" a lot that my Mom, who was diagnosed with Alzheimer's, would become paranoid in her forgetfulness, maybe mean, and even an invalid lost in her body. But God was merciful, took her home early, and I worried for naught. I want to say 'thank you'! to Stephen for helping me move out of the pit of worry and anxiety and even see God's mercy in my Mom's death. I am humbled and grateful that God loves me and delivered this book to me at just the right time!

-Janet Bledsoe

Stephen Scoggins knocks it out of the park with his tell-all book. The book is an extremely easy read and feels like you are having a conversation with the man himself. After reading, it definitely lit a spark under me and gave me a "why not?" mentality. The stories give you great insight on how when you combine positivity and faith, you can be anything you want to be. I fully recommend!

-Jake Jablonski

At times in our lives we know we are missing something, we are looking for an answer, we wonder if our prayers even get through the roof, get your hands on this and really read it, you will know God answers prayers even the ones we wonder about. It will lift you up, make you a more understanding of God's time and His will not ours. I placed it on the couch seat when guest are coming in so they have to ask me about it as they wish to move it and sit down and it is hitting home with several folks that are searching for answers. Thank you Stephen for the "Journey", I enjoyed the walk.

-Judson Walton

Stephen Scoggins "The Journey Principles" is a must read. Using an autobiographical approach, the author clearly details and explains the key fundamental principles to achieve a good life that has purpose and value. Stephen Scoggins not only gives us an excellent faith perspective but also clearly explains the world view of his 10 key principles. Overall this book was an easy, enjoyable read that really helped reinforce my faith and hope. I truly feel blessed to have this book as a resource that I can often use in the future to help me on my own life journey. I will definitely keep it on my resource list.

-Hugh Bray

The
Journey
Principles™

YOUR JOURNEY, GOD'S PRINCIPLES

Our Social Media QR Codes

www.stephenscoggins.com

Facebook

Twitter

Instagram